DEVELOPING YOUTH WORK

Developing Youth Work

Informal Education, Mutual Aid and Popular Practice

Mark Smith

Open University Press
Milton Keynes · Philadelphia

Open University Press
Open University Educational Enterprises Limited
12 Cofferidge Close
Stony Stratford
Milton Keynes MK11 1BY

and
242 Cherry Street
Philadelphia, PA 19106, USA

First Published 1988

British Library Cataloguing in Publication Data

Smith, Mark, *1950–*
    Developing youth work: informal education, mutual aid and
    popular practice.
    1. Great Britain. Youth work
    I. Title
    362.7'0941

    ISBN 0–335–15835–8
    ISBN 0–335–15834–X (pbk.)

Library of Congress Cataloging-in-Publication Data

Smith, Mark, 1950 June 25–
    Developing youth work: informal education, mutual aid, and
popular practice / Mark Smith.
        p.   cm.
        Bibliography: p.
        Includes index.
    1. Social work with youth——Great Britain. 2. Non-formal
education——Great Britain. I. Title
    HV1441.G7S55   1988
    362.7'042——dc19

    ISBN 0–335–15835–8
    ISBN 0–335–15834–X (pbk.)

Typeset by Colset Pte Ltd, Singapore
Printed in Great Britain by Oxford University Press

Contents

List of Abbreviations

BYV	Birmingham Young Volunteers
CARF	Campaign Against Racism and Fascism
CETYCW	Council for the Education and Training of Youth and Community Workers
COS	Charity Organizations Society (*now* The Family Welfare Association)
CP	Community Programme (MSC)
DES	Department of Education and Science
DHSS	Department of Health and Social Security
FE	Further Education
GFS	Girls' Friendly Society
GRE	Grant-related Expenditure
GREA	Grant-related Expenditure Assessment
HE	Higher Education
HMI	Her Majesty's Inspectorate (Education)
ILEA	Inner London Education Authority
IT	Intermediate Treatment
LCC	London County Council
LEA	Local Education Authority
MSC	Manpower Services Commission
NACYS	National Advisory Council for the Youth Service
NAYC	National Association of Youth Clubs (*now* Youth Clubs UK)
NCSS	National Council of Social Service (*now* National Council of Voluntary Organizations)
NIYWA	Northern Ireland Youth Workers' Association
NISW	National Institute of Social Work
NYB	National Youth Bureau

SCOYO	Standing Conference of Youth Organizations (Northern Ireland)
YMCA	Young Men's Christian Association
YOP	Youth Opportunities Programme
YSIC	Youth Service Information Centre
YTS	Youth Training Scheme
YWCA	Young Women's Christian Association

Preface

This book began life in 1982 as an attempt to construct a coherent and distinctive understanding of youth work. While it would be nice to claim that the thinking reported in these pages has matured and developed through constant reflection over the intervening years, the truth is that it has had a stuttering existence, competing with all sorts of other demands. What follows, therefore, has to be seen as 'work-in-progress' and is offered in the hope that it may further stimulate thinking about the practice of youth work and informal education.

Much of the thinking represented here has been greatly enhanced as a result of collaborating with Tony Jeffs in the editing of a series of books about discrete aspects of youth work. One book sought to encourage practitioner theorizing about practice (1987a), another explored youth work's place in welfare (1988a), and the third examined practice which addressed social division and inequality (1988b). The process of editing these collections confirmed the need for a text which attempted to provide a rationale and method for youth work.

The long time span involved in the writing of this book has meant that ideas have been tried out on a large number of people. Among the principal sufferers have been my colleagues and students at the YMCA National College – to them my thanks. Again, very special thanks are due to Tony Jeffs – while what follows is 'all my own work', elements of the book, and in particular Chapter 4, could not have been written without those joint efforts. Chris, Alex and Christopher Rogers have given great support. In addition, the questions 'when's tea?', 'what's for tea?' and 'why don't you write a real book like Len Deighton?' have helped to keep the project in proportion. Thanks are also due to *Youth and Policy* for allowing me to use a small amount of material which originally appeared in one of their occasional papers (M. Smith, 1987).

Finally, I would like to dedicate this book to Dorothy and Harry Smith. Much of the subject matter relates to their history. They first met nearly 50 years ago as members in a youth club, later ran one as volunteers, and still later sat on the management committees of various youth organizations. In them, and many thousands like them, lies youth work's strength and future.

Mark Smith

Note on Quotations

Readers may notice that I have left quotations in their original gendered state. It is not always clear what the writers implied by their use of 'he' and 'his'!

All emphases in quotations are as in the original.

Introduction

So much of what is said about youth work either seeks to conceal or is the product of lazy or rhetorical thinking. The ahistorical, apolitical and anti-intellectual attitude of many in this area has meant that practice is peculiarly prone to influence by moral panics, fads and fashions. As such, the work is further threatened both by the development of very different forms of practice directed at many of the areas that youth workers have claimed as their own, and by the growing diversity of organizational settings in which workers are located. Yet youth work has much to offer and certain strands of practice have the potential to make a major contribution to the well-being of young people. If youth workers are to make that contribution and retain a unique identity and distinctive forms of working, they must address a number of fundamental philosophical and political questions, and develop the necessary theory.

In what follows I hope something of the potential of youth work and how it may be developed is demonstrated. I have attempted to place youth work in time and context, explore actual as against idealized practice, and set out basic principles. This may sound ambitious, but the time seemed right for something 'big'; it is some 20 years since the last attempts (Davies and Gibson, 1967; Milson (1970)) to reconceptualize youth work practice in this way.

The book begins with an examination of the development of youth work and the crisis it now faces. Chapter 1 explores some of the key factors that led to attention being focused on youth and, in particular, on the behaviour and attitudes of working-class young people. I have attempted to show how the notion of adolescence came to be important and has to be seen as a bourgeois construction.

From this I chart the 'discovery' of bourgeois youth work and the forms that it took.

With the development of modern leisure forms, the emergence of organic approaches to youth work and changes in what the middle classes expected of intervention, there was a significant shift in the generalized character of practice in the 1930s and 1940s. The leadership and membership of many clubs and units became recognizably working class and what might be termed popular youth work became established. It is the making of this practice which is the focus of Chapter 2.

Chapter 3 explores the clusters of key ideas that appear to inform the ways that youth workers see their tasks. Six broad bodies of customs, thoughts and practices that are recognizable in what workers and commentators have said and written about youth work over the last century are then suggested. The durability of form within these provides some sense of stability and legitimacy, while at the same time allowing considerable difference and change.

In Chapter 4, I examine the nature of the crisis facing youth work and the Youth Service. Britain has become a more unequal and divided society, in part because of economic recession and restructuring, but also as a result of government policy. It has been argued that the social condition of young people has altered. Within this context, three broad sets of interrelated questions are seen as central to youth work's crisis. First, the rationale and practice of welfare has come under attack. Secondly, the relative development of other forms of provision for young people, both public and commercial, has pushed the Youth Service into something of a corner. Thirdly, the lack of attention to theory and purpose has left youth workers vulnerable to a range of questions concerning their practice. While it is possible that the Youth Service will wither away, there are vibrant strands of practice which will continue to evolve, whatever the administrative categories policy makers may use to handle them.

From this I then examine in Chapter 5, the notion of social education and its deficiencies as a rationale and 'method' in work with young people. In particular I question the usefulness of notions such as 'growing up' and 'maturity'. The personalist orientation of much of its practice is also examined. I argue that social education should be abandoned as a way of conceptualizing the aims and methods of youth work.

What then is to be the purpose of youth work? Chapter 6 suggests that practitioners should set out to enable individuals to pursue autonomously their own well-being. In particular, they should seek to enlarge young people's understanding of their own well-being so that they may weigh their own needs with those of others, help them to display civic courage, and enable them to gain the knowledge, skills and disposition necessary to think and act politically. Not only does this represent an argument for a basic shift towards educative practice, but also asserts that the primary focus in youth work should move away from a near-exclusive concern with the self and immediate others.

Having established what might be the purpose of youth work, I go on to examine informal education as a method. At the centre of such an approach is the idea of a critical dialogue between workers and learners, and among workers themselves and learners themselves. Finally, in Chapter 8, I explore some of the central questions associated with the development of popular youth work and the implementation of good practice. I suggest that major advances can be made by workers themselves. In particular, I argue that emphasis should be placed upon approaches which stress mutual aid and self-organization.

These conclusions cannot pretend to be anything other than tentative. The understandings developed are, to some extent, confined by the existing vocabulary of youth work and informal education as that language has become mine. If practitioners want to develop practice for good ends, then the words they use to describe what they do and why they do it will require careful interrogation. For this to happen they will have to engage in a critical dialogue with each other and with young people. In the end, the exercise youth workers may have to set themselves is the creation of a new vocabulary concerning informal work with young people. This may even involve renaming themselves.

Chapter 1

Enter Youth Workers

Before large-scale industrialization, the now familiar ways of differentiating people according to age were not widespread. The emergence of the concepts of childhood and adolescence appear to have corresponded with the development of the capitalist system of production (Thane, 1981), although there is no simple relationship between the two (Springhall, 1986: 25). While for most people there was a period of infancy, when the child was dependent on adults, modern 'childhood' was something that arguably emerged in the sixteenth or seventeenth centuries within middle- and upper-class families (Aries, 1962; Pollock, 1983). Within pre-industrial European economies children were working in the home or around it by about age four or five. Many young women and men had left home by puberty to work as servants or apprentices in other households. Thus, children were quickly absorbed into the productive process and would mix with adults in both work and social situations.

As the middle and upper class came to understand childhood as a time of innocence and preparation for adulthood, the technical demands of the economy produced the need for ever-longer periods of training and apprenticeship. Worries about children's experiences of work and their behaviour on urban streets led to a range of interventions and legislation aimed at creating the conditions for childhood. Attention also turned to youth. In an often quoted phrase, Musgrove has claimed that the adolescent was invented at the same time as the steam engine, 'the principal architect of the latter was Watt in 1765, of the former Rousseau in 1762' (Musgrove, 1964: 33). In Rousseau's view puberty was a second birth. It was then that 'man really enters upon life; henceforth no human passion is a stranger to him' (Rousseau, 1911: 173). However, it was not until the late nineteenth century that 'adolescence' came into anything like widespread usage in the United Kingdom (Gillis, 1974: 95–132). Like 'childhood', 'adolescence', as far as young men at least were concerned, could be viewed as being 'an innovation of, by, and for the middle class' (Macleod, 1983: xv). The aspirations of the middle class concerning their offspring then became the template by which the experience of others was later to be judged.

Two interlinking elements are pictured as crucial to the widespread application of the concept to working class young people – the development of compulsory schooling and changes in the economy (Walvin, 1982: 186–92). The effect of these was apparently to create or highlight a time of delay and discontinuity which could be labelled as a peculiar property of youth. Throughout the nineteenth century schooling expanded, first in voluntary and Ragged schools and Dame schools, then by the state following the 1870 Education Act. By 1893 the school leaving age was 11 and by 1899 it had risen to 12. This, combined with increased efforts to enforce attendance, had a considerable impact: first, by pulling children 'off the streets', it transferred the problem of their control to the classroom (Humphries, 1981); and secondly, while there may have been seasonal, part-time and indeed casual employment, children had their access to the symbols and benefits of adult economic life postponed. Their importance to the labour market had become marginal.

At the same time, there were changes in technology and in the economy which gave rise to different types of employment opportunities for young people, particularly in urban areas. For instance, large numbers of young men found employment in the various occupations that emerged with the growing complex of distributive and administrative functions. Frequently these jobs were 'reserved' for people in their teens; paying adult rates for van boys and messenger boys was seen as uneconomic. With young people being forced to leave such employment in their late teens, a discontinuity emerged between juvenile and adult work. This entered political debates at the turn of the century and was expressed in a number of books and articles concerned with 'The Boy Labour Problem' (Urwick, 1904; Russell, 1905; Bray, 1907). The moral panic engendered by large numbers of children on the streets had apparently been replaced by one involving young people (Pearson, 1983: 58–62). In addition, between 1890 and 1910 the accuracy of national statistics concerning juvenile crime improved substantially, and these changes were mistakenly used as evidence of a massive increase in crime. This judgement was further enhanced by increased action being taken against certain types of 'crime', e.g. drunkenness, gambling, malicious mischief, loitering, begging and dangerous play (Muncie, 1984: 40).

Little ladies at home

Some young women were also observed to be involved in a street problem of another kind. In many larger cities and towns there was a flourishing trade in child prostitution, due in part to the incidence of venereal disease (young women were less likely to be infected), to the cult of the 'little girl' and sexual fantasies around young children, and to the appalling social and financial position of many working-class families. In response to the work of journalists such as W.T. Stead and campaigners such as Josephine Butler there was a considerable public demand for the Government to act. Thus, in 1885, Parliament passed the Criminal Law Amendment Act which raised the age of consent to 16 and made it an offence to procure a women under the age of 21.

A number of middle-class women were also worried about the conditions faced by young women in domestic service and in the factories and sweated labour shops, and still others were appalled by young women's experiences in the home.

Many a girl who works hard all day can never get to rest early, because she has to wait till all the family go to bed. She does not know what it is to have a solitary or a quiet half hour. She lives in a chronic condition of nervous exhaustion. (Pethick, 1898: 113)

In one sense the experiences of these young women was hidden. They were not seen to be quite the problem that young men were and, as Nava has argued, the control and supervision of young women has always been in the home (1984: 1). Yet home life was also undergoing a restructuring.

The separation of the home from work, changing rhythms of working life and demands for different forms of skill had their impact upon the shape of household life. Some of the changes were consciously promoted; for example, the middle class through their economic and political power were able to influence significantly the shape of, and power relations within, the family. Their ideals and beliefs came to dominate nineteenth-century legislation and ideology:

The central belief that emerged . . . was that of a male

breadwinner gaining a livelihood through work and maintaining his female (and child) dependants within the home. . . . In this view, husband and wife were the archetype, but father and child, brother and sister, uncle and niece, master and servant reproduced the relationships of clientage and dependency. (Davidoff, 1976, quoted in Gittins, 1985: 31)

Gittins goes on to comment that this was not just a family ideology, but also a gender ideology. It was a careful and deliberate attempt to reorganize the relations between sexes according to middle-class ways and values and then define the outcome as somehow being natural. These changes both affected the way in which young men and women experienced these institutions and how young people were perceived by adults, or at least by middle-class adults. Thus, both young men and women were viewed as problematic and they had to be fitted into the new social and industrial order that the reformers wished to see. Indisciplined, dangerously independent and precocious, their 'personality' was a matter of grave concern (Hendricks, 1986: 33–9). The family was to play its part, with women undertaking the major productive role therein and providing the conditions for the men's activities in the world. In addition, women were to provide a reserve army of labour, to be used as the economy demanded their services.

The making of modern leisure

By the second half of the nineteenth century, allied to changes in work and the structures of household life, leisure began to take a form that is recognizable today. Four key factors have been identified by Cunningham as influencing its shape (1980: 140–87). First is the operation of the market forces of supply and demand. In response to the growing wealth of the working class a considerable commercial sector developed. This included the growth of various forms of variety theatres and penny gaffs, public houses, travel opportunities such as day excursions, popular literature such as the 'penny dreadfuls', and sports of various kinds. Secondly, these market forces were clearly modified by the attachment of the working class to forms of leisure created in the first half of the nineteenth century and before. This included loyalty to various games and sports and to the public house, the usage of which was already fragmented by gender. Thirdly, increased provision by government and charity organizations in the name of 'rational recreation' led to the spread of public parks, libraries, wash houses and museums. Finally, market forces were also affected by a growing view of the dangers of leisure and these were expressed in calls to control leisure activities and to privatize a number in the home. Furthermore, not only did leisure become privatized, but within Western society a particular concept of the individual developed, and this increasing differentiation of people has subsequently been mirrored by a mounting specialism in leisure pursuits (Rojek, 1985: 18–25).

The middle class already had a degree of control over the experience of work, schooling and other forms of incarceration, including hospitals, poor houses and prisons. Considerable effort was also expended in an attempt to cultivate correct attitudes and behaviour within the churches. What appeared to elude the middle class was any influence over the private world of the working class home and the 'dangerous' pastimes they enjoyed. There was an abhorrence of 'brutal' sports, cheap entertainments, drinking and gambling, all of which were seen to be ungodly, as posing a threat to order and as a reflection of the moral failure of the working classes. Leisure was 'that dangerous time for working boys – the time between leaving work and retiring to bed' (Greenwood, 1869: 44). For it was in that space and in the pursuits undertaken, that many of the middle classes' worst fears about the working-class young were manifest: 'they were said to be completely free from restraint or guidance; they mixed with friends of their own choosing (and often with undesirable adults); and they were thriftless with money' (Hendricks, 1986: 33). The leisure activities of the working-class young were therefore to be singled out for attention.

Threats from within and without

As if the dangerous personality of working-class young people were not enough, other forces were also at work. The growth of working-class political organization was seen by many in the middle class as heralding a period of intensified class conflict. Socialism, like Chartism before it, was perceived as a threat to stability (Simon, 1965: 60). Crucially, it can be argued that something akin to a remaking of the working class took place in the years between 1870 and 1900; that the solidarity and organizational strength achieved in earlier struggles were:

> channelled into trade union activity and eventually into a political party based on that activity and its goals. The distinctiveness of a working-class way of life was enormously

accentuated. Its separateness and impermeability were now reflected in a dense and inward-looking culture, whose effect was both to emphasize the distance of the working class from the classes above it and to articulate its position within an apparently permanent social hierarchy. (Stedman Jones, 1983: 236-7)

These interrelated developments can be seen as signifying a shift in the central forms of working-class activity. The dangers of this were not lost upon the middle class. Later, William Smith, the founder of the Boys Brigade, while defending the training and discipline brought by war, claimed he was 'not at all sure that there were not elements of just as much evil . . . and bitterness of spirit in the industrial wars between class and class which many signs point to as the conflicts of the future but which, like other wars, may have their part to play in the progress of the race' (quoted by Springhall *et al.*, 1983: 20). Young people were sometimes pictured as being parti-cularly susceptible to the appeals of extremists, a point taken up by Baden-Powell:

> Extreme ideas are seldom much good; if you look them up in history you will see almost always they have been tried before somewhere. The Socialists are right in wishing to get money more evenly distributed. . . . But they go the wrong way to work; they want to fight all other people to get themselves up, instead of joining in with everybody in doing a great thing for the whole country by a way which is fair and good for all.
> More thrift rather than a change in government will bring money to all. And a strong united Europe, where all are helpful and patriotic will bring us power, peace and prosperity such as no Socialist dream could do. (quoted by Rosenthal, 1986: 183)

In contrast, some, particularly from dissenting traditions, felt able to strike a rather more conciliatory note. For example, Dr John Gladstone prepared a paper for the YMCA in 1891 on its 'Attitude with regard to Socialism', in which he admitted that 'the sufferings that oppress whole classes of men baffle the efforts of individuals; they must be grappled with by organized co-operation or the compulsion of the government' (Binfield, 1973: 375).

To fears of, and debates about socialism and working-class political organization were added concerns about Britain's ability to maintain the Empire. This had particular implications for domestic stability and wealth:

> The exploitation and degradation of the colonial working class

was an indispensable requirement in maintaining the standard of living of the British working class. . . . The British economy is really a 'parasitic economy' dependent on colonial revenues for its maintenance. (Ramdin 1987: 63)

The 'issue' of Ireland further 'condensed anxieties about the British imperial position as no other could, for if the Empire were to be dislocated at its very centre its prospects looked bleak' (Hall and Schwarz, 1985: 13). The South African war of the 1890s revealed 'both the poor physical condition of the recruits and the inefficiency of their military commanders' (Springhall, 1977: 14). Yet it was not only war on the physical front that was causing concern, but also the emergence of other industrial and trading nations, in particular the United States and Germany, and the possibility of 'economic defeat'. Therefore, due to the experience of the Boer War combined with fears about the British economy, there was 'a demand for state and voluntary welfare measures designed to increase "national efficiency", in the contemporary phrase, among influential social groups who previously had been hostile or indifferent to social issues' (Thane, 1982: 61).

There was also a growing shift from fears about the 'fitness' of the population, to the aspiration to breed and educate an 'imperial race' (Donald, 1985: 223). This can be seen in attitudes towards 'immigrants'. By 1900, while Irish and Jewish immigration had dwindled, these groups had settled in the cities:

concentrated in small inner districts, in a pattern which foreshadowed later waves of immigration, not only through overcrowded housing and competition with older residents for already poorly paid work, but also in their uneven path to social integration, marked by considerable social prejudice and political protest. (Thompson, 1975: 42)

At the same time the small black communities adjoining major ports were also experiencing considerable deprivation and discrimination (Law, 1981: 24-7). Racism, the 'principal handmaiden to Empire' (Fryer, 1984: 165) was to be found in the attitude of the middle class and in that of the organized working class. Nationalist and Imperial fears gave some stimulus to arguments for racial purity. The Eugenicists advocated measures to restrain the mentally and physically weak from reproducing, offered some credence to the growth in anti-semitism, and fed the hostility that led to restrictions upon Jewish immigration in the Aliens Act 1905 (Thane, 1982: 59-60). For the middle class these indeed did seem dangerous times.

Psychology – the final piece of the jigsaw

Middle-class reformers already had access to common sense explanations of the problems faced by young men and women. For instance, Eagar talks of early youth workers looking 'to what became of the growing boy who was no longer a child but was not yet a man. They discerned an intermediate age, plastic, impressionable, perilous and formative' (1953: 21). However, there now arrived a scientific justification for such work with young people and an 'explanation' of why working-class young people might be considered as lacking the potential for intellectual and emotional development. The conceptualization of adolescence which initially emerged under the influence of writers such as Hall (1904, 1906) and Slaughter (1911) provided a key means by which a pathological picture of working-class young people could be sustained.

Hall argued that people pass through a number of stages in their development and that these stages correspond to those that occurred during human evolution. In this he drew heavily on Darwinism:

> Thus each individual re-lived the development of the human race from animal-like primitivism (childhood) through periods of savagery (adolescence) to finally achieve civilized ways of life (adulthood). Within such a psychobiological framework he thus argued that 'adolescence is pre-eminently the criminal age' and that 'criminals are like overgrown children'. (Muncie, 1984: 42)

Hall emphasized adolescence as a time of storm and stress and laid particular stress upon the overriding importance of puberty within adolescence. His ideas about adolescence were, in many respects, 'simply a culmination of views that had been around in a less systematic way for much of the nineteenth century' (Springhall, 1986: 29).

While much of Hall's major work on adolescence was devoted to the study of young men, he did discuss female adolescence as well. At the time of publication, and subsequently, the book aroused considerable fury among feminists:

> For the boy, [adolescence] was a time of ambition, growth and challenge. For the girl, it was a time of instability; a dangerous phase when she needed self protection from society. During adolescence, boys grew towards self knowledge. Girls on the other hand, could never really obtain self knowledge. They

could never hope to understand much of themselves or the motives for their conduct, for their lives were ruled by 'deep unconscious instinct', and a girl's self consciousness was only the "reflected knowledge that others had to offer". Women, Hall insisted, never really outgrew their adolescence and this constituted their charm, their eternal womanliness. (Dyhouse, 1981: 122)

Hall's work was disseminated through a large number of other people's writings and in texts directly aimed at youth workers and teachers. For example, Russell and Rigby (1908) were clearly influenced by him, as were key figures in Scouting and Woodcraft such as Ernest Westlake and John Hargrave (Rosenthal, 1986: 242, 250). His attempt to refute the possibilities of female autonomy dove-tailed with earlier Victorian concepts of femininity and the family. That idea of femininity represented economic and intellectual dependency and saw service and self-sacrifice as defining features of womanhood.

The more generalized use of the notion of adolescence, and the way in which a number of behaviours could be thus attributed to a phase young people were going through, helped to shift attention away from material inequality as a way of explaining the position of young people. Juvenile delinquency could be explained as the 'natural attribute of adolescence'. Lack of parental guidance combined with 'troublesome adolescence' remained the dominant form of explanation of deliquency up until the 1950s.

Working class adolescents were thought to be most likely to display delinquent and rebellious characteristics during this 'storm and stress' period in the life cycle because it was widely assumed that working class parents exercised inadequate control over brutal adolescent instincts. (Humphries, 1981: 17)

The new consciousness of 'adolescence' was thus considerably enhanced by the efforts of psychologists. While some may have stuck tenaciously to the epithet 'youth', the codification of thinking that had taken place in the name of adolescence could hardly have escaped them. Those who saw it as their duty or job to intervene in the lives of young people, now had a suitable vocabulary of scientific terms with which to carry forward their intentions.

The new provision

Armed with the new language of social science, and stung by fears of social disruption and imperial decline, significant elements of the middle class devoted some of their energies to charitable efforts. Perhaps the largest single inspiration was evangelicalism. Similarly, the efforts of the Jewish community, especially after the influx of refugees from the Russian pogroms, made an impact upon welfare thinking and provision. Much of the financial support came from well-to-do middle-class families, although lower income groups also made contributions (Thane, 1982: 21). Throughout the mid-Victorian period there had been a steady rise in the proportion of people in the UK population engaged in middle-class occupations. Those engaged in trade, commerce, literature, science and education increased significantly (Best, 1979: 104–11). However, there is a danger of treating this grouping as if it was homogeneous. While the use of class as an explanatory tool had developed, and class consciousness had grown, responses to social questions were varied. Thus, for example, we might wish to distinguish an educated professional sector from 'the mass of small employers, shopkeepers and house-owners at one end of the spectrum, and from substantial merchants, bankers and the City elite at the other' (Stedman Jones, 1984: xv).

Much of the charitable effort was centred in large cities where there was a significant middle-class presence close to the forms of deprivation and 'problems' that so alarmed their sensibilities. London, especially the East End, became the site for many forms of philanthropic intervention. The composition of London's middle class was skewed towards professions such as law, medicine, the church, the military and the civil service, groups which were of considerable importance in determining the formation of characteristic attitudes towards the problem of poverty. The absence of substantial, direct economic links between these particular groupings of the rich and the poor, as for example between employer and employee, can be seen as explaining the importance of charitable activity in London, 'both as a mode of interpreting the behaviour of the poor and as a means of attempting to control them' (Stedman Jones, 1984: 240).

There does appear to be something of a sea-change in the attitude of key groups to the notion of intervention – particularly with the 'casual poor'. The London dock strike of 1889 and the riots of 1886, along with the concerns already outlined earlier, provoked the 'intellectual assault which began to be mounted against *laissez faire* both from the right and the left in the 1880s' (Stedman Jones, 1984: 297). Nevertheless, while the extent of government action concerning perceived social problems undoubtedly increased from

1870 to 1900, it was limited when compared with the demands for action and the nature of the problems themselves. The prevailing anti-interventionist ideology in relation to the state undoubtedly played a part, but other factors were also at work. Perhaps the central factor related to the importance attached to low taxation, especially within the Liberal Party. Such a commitment 'remained an obstacle to central government action and was actually worsened by the high cost of the Boer War which opened in 1899' (Thane, 1982: 45). The state, both local and central, was envisaged as providing a 'safety net', a net which operated to a large extent through the Poor Law. Beyond this there were incursions into welfare, such as in education, but by-and-large such works were to be left to voluntary organizations.

It was against this backdrop that youth work was developing Youths' Clubs and Youths' Institutes appeared in the late 1850s and early 1860s (Eagar, 1953: 161) – the first Jewish youth organization of which there is any convincing record is the Leman Street Girls' Club in 1883 (Bunt, 1975: 11), the Girls' Friendly Society was founded in 1874 and by 1885 had 821 branches (Dyhouse, 1981: 108), and handbooks on club work appeared in 1889 (Pelham) and 1890 (Stanley). By 1884, Pelham reported that the growth of Working-boys' Clubs and Institutes had been remarkable. 'Such an institution is now considered part of the parochial machinery in every populous district. There are now about 300 parochial institutions for young men and boys in the Diocese of London and about 50 others not connected with any church. Twenty years ago there were probably not a score' (quoted in Eagar, 1953: 240). Many of the London boys' clubs not connected with a church were closely tied in with public school and university missions. Significantly, it was in the 1880s that the first 'youth organization', the Young Men's Christian Association, initiated in 1844, began to make a mass impact (Simon, 1965: 62).

From the mid-nineteenth century on, youth work was to assume many guises although Jeffs, among others, has suggested that with the passing of the 1870 Education Act and the gradual addition of other welfare legislation to the statute book, there was a significant shift in its style and emphasis. With schools apparently offering basic instruction and other agencies material and other welfare assistance, many clubs and youth organizations now chose to concern themselves overwhelmingly with 'the inculcation of intangible social and spiritual values amongst their clients rather than in improving their material well-being' (Jeffs, 1979: 4). Thus, youth work could be understood not as an effort to further the natural intellectual development of the person, but as a means of producing subjectivity. It helped to secure often 'unconscious structures which make people responsive to certain representations' (Donald, 1985: 241).

How were young people to be attracted by sponsors and workers to these places of improvement in their 'own' time? The answer was to be recreation, i.e. in return for an opportunity for some amusement, young people would have to submit themselves for 'improvement'.

> They have their special wants and dangers, which call for such an agency as the Youths' Institute. Their peculiar wants are evening recreation, companionship, an entertaining but healthy literature, useful instruction, and a strong guiding influence to lead them onward and upward socially and morally; their dangers are, the long evenings consequent upon early closing, the unrestraint they are allowed at home, the temptation of the streets and of their time of life, and a little money at the bottom of their pockets. (Sweatman, 1863: 42)

Working-class culture was a primary target for workers' actions:

> Children required salvation from the vices of their parent culture; . . . a second set of evils lay in the wiles of gambling, moral laxity, the 'animal excitement' of theatres . . . and the curse of drink. Clubs, then, wished to direct working-class leisure into respectable channels, with either a religious or military bias or both. They also existed to act as a focal point for loyalties. To their organizers, the closed nature of working class society evidenced a self-centred and selfish perspective on life. (Blanch, 1979: 105)

Mixed up in these two accounts are two key traditions of conceptualizing working-class youth: theories of mass culture and theories of deprivation. The former view stressed change in the economic and social systems and the way they undermined many traditional values and weakened any collective or individual sense of purpose. Working-class young people, whether through their structural position, lack of experience, immaturity or ignorance, were thus viewed as particularly vulnerable to the effects of a mass society (Humphries, 1981: 3–14). On the other hand, there have been those who have articulated concerns about working-class youth through theories of deprivation. Here a common form was a belief that they had a 'hereditary lack of potential for intellectual and emotional development' (Humphries, 1981: 14). Other forms have tended to focus on cultural deprivation, the belief that that allegedly restricted linguistic and conceptual codes, authoritarian or inconsistent discipline and low expectations of achievement contributed to a culture of poverty.

Jewish youth work also expressed these concerns. Bunt argues that it was the extreme squalor and the perception of the 'temptations of the street' that led to the establishment of many early Jewish Youth Clubs. Significantly, one of the key elements of the work was the 'anglicizing' of the children of new Jewish immigrants. The intention was to provide a new culture of 'Jewish Englishness'. Central elements of Jewish culture were to be retained in such a way as to ensure its maintenance and, at the same time, the new immigrants were encouraged into ways of life that the Jewish middle class saw as appropriate to British society.

If young people were to be 'improved' then they would have to be taken out of the home or street or any other environment that contributed to that which was offensive to middle-class mores. It was necessary to provide an environment that would create a strong identity to the youth organization and its ideology, and to the other members. In doing so it was only then possible to transcend the cultures so offensive to the middle-class philanthropists. At first the two strands of amusement and improvement were set against each other, particularly in work with boys. Later, they were frequently joined in the notion of 'improving amusement'. For example, many of the London boys' clubs, particularly those under the aegis of public school missions, placed an emphasis on games. In part this was in response to the lack of opportunities for sports in Board Schools and at work. The muscular Christianity of Kingsley and Hughes was well adapted to club life (Simon, 1965: 68).

Sponsors of early clubs and youth provision recognized that if they were to safeguard the values and institutions they themselves believed in, then young people would have to be socialized into seeing the world as they did. There was not total agreement about what should be done. Within the middle class, there evolved competing understandings and these were reflected, to some extent, in the different traditions of practice which emerged. Inevitably, differing experiences and intellectual and moral positions were to find expression in debates such as that between Smith of the Boys' Brigade and Baden-Powell, or in the feminist and collectivist analysis that emanated from parts of the girls' work movement.

Within the girls' club movement there initially appeared to be a concentration rather more on amusement than education or leadership. 'We must turn to and provide for the girls that which their parents truly say they cannot provide – healthy and safe recreations, amusements and occupation for their leisure hours' (Stanley, 1890: 14). Yet there were those who sought rather more. Montagu desired to correct the 'tendency to individualism and self-seeking which are produced by workshop life' (1904: 246). She saw clubs stimulating 'the members' power of self-control and their sense of responsibility and widen(ing) the average conception of happiness' (Montagu, 1904: 247). Pethick reported on her experience of girls work in the 1890s:

> The conditions, not only of the home, but of the factory or workshop had to be taken into account. It became our business to study the industrial question as it affected the girls' employments, the hours, the wages, and the conditions. And we had also to give them a conscious part to take in the battle that is being fought for the workers, and will not be won until it is loyally fought by the workers as well. (Pethick, 1898: 104)

The effectiveness of the new provision was, as might be expected, limited. For example, while clubs might have exploited the need for recreation among working-class adolescents, and combined this with their being vehicles for a conservative ideology, they did not necessarily attract large numbers. As White comments upon one Jewish club in the early 1900s:

> The Butler Street Club, for example, sought 'to lure girls from the streets, the Penny Gaffs and the musical halls', but it succeeded in luring less than 200 girls away from pursuits unacceptable to the middle class. The stronger attractions of that culture of the streets and the musical hall and the cinema held greater sway over the youth of Rothschild Buildings than the given culture of the club. (White, 1980: 190)

Part of the reason for the failure to attract working-class young people lies in the tension between social provision and improving aims. First, the grand claim:

> Their primary object, the keeping of lads off the streets, has gradually grown into the altogether wider and larger conception of moulding their characters and physique until the elements be so mixed in them that Nature may proclaim them men. The making of men! That in a word, is the ideal aimed at and . . . [we] hope to show that it is not altogether unfulfilled. (Russell and Rigby, 1908: 22)

Then some of the tensions are revealed in what Russell and Rigby described as the three objects of boys' clubs. Recreation (the compelling force which brings members to the club), education (comprising the whole physical, moral and mental training of lads), and religion (comprehending all the impalpable influences which give a club a grip on its members and tend to awaken their higher nature) (Russell and Rigby, 1908: 19–20). Substitute temperance for religion and we have the three fronts upon which Solly envisaged working-class improvement would proceed (Bailey, 1987: 178). These he claimed were like a three-legged stool, remove one and the whole project collapses. The early reformers fashioned the three legs, but appeared incapable of getting them the same length. 'Striking a balance between easy congeniality and earnest improvement – "How to steer between weak tea and good behaviour and a rollicking free and easy" – was a social exercise for which the bourgeois philanthropist was ill equipped' (Bailey, 1987: 179); a position further hampered by a lack of relevant commercial and managerial expertise and 'historic capital of social skills' in working-class leisure provision (Bailey, 1987).

Similarly, if the intention of middle-class workers and sponsors was to show the underprivileged how to live, then, as Gillis has commented, the slum dwellers had some lessons of their own to teach. A clergyman who had been active in the Oxford Men's and Lads' Institute in the 1880s remembered:

> The boys were very good fellows, but they regarded the Institute as an opening for permanent 'Town and Gown' conflict, and naturally began at once to measure their strength against those who had come to civilize and instruct them. Classes were started, but often terminated prematurely; the scholars would turn off the gas, stick pins in their teacher, and break up the furniture. (quoted by Gillis, 1974: 174–5)

Stanley provides graphic accounts of similar problems;

> Two bigger girls who were sitting happily at work . . . while a story was read to them, suddenly quarrelled about a thimble, and in a passion one girl threw the table over, the others mad with excitement began to act in the wildest, utterly indescrib-able fashion. . . . The horrified workers found the lower room in still worse confusion. Boys were banging at the shutters and door, the girls inside shouting and singing, and even fighting, slates, books and sewing being used as missiles. . . . One of the ladies went to speak to the lads outside, and one threw his cap in, and getting his foot in the doorway prevented the door

being closed. Remonstrances were of no use. (Stanley, 1890: 195–6)

Given the wide discrepancy between the need of the girls as perceived by the organizers and as perceived by the girls, 'it is no wonder that the most successful clubs tended to be led by a charismatic and devoted leader or else conducted through a process of self-selection that eliminated all but the quietest and most submissive members' (Vicinus, 1985: 233). In this clash of cultures and of interests it is perhaps not surprising that it was the sons and daughters of the middle classes and upper-working classes who predominantly joined these early organizations. This tendency was generally true of the whole rational recreation movement where, 'in their concern to expedite improvement, reformers frequently rejected the osmosis of example-setting and adopted an autocratic manner which alienated workingmen' (Bailey, 1987: 179). Humphries has also charted the resistance of working-class young people to the various attempts to improve them. He reports 'larking about' in the numerous youth organizations attached to churches and in the various uniformed organizations. Indeed, the lack of success of the boys clubs in bolstering up church attendances and the problems that arose when they did turn up is seen by at least one commentator as being a significant factor in the Anglican Church's retreat from such work (Dawes, 1975: 100–101).

There will be drill

During the 1880s, other more structured forms of work appeared. The Boys' Brigade was the first to mix drill, athleticism and the wearing of a uniform, and it was later followed by a number of similar organizations including the Church Lads' Brigade (1891), the Jewish Lads' Brigade (1895) and the Catholic Boys' Brigade (1896). The outdoor healthiness and social imperialism of Scouting appeared in its organized form in 1908. Blanch (1979) suggests three main strands of nationalist attitudes which link these early male organizations. First, the idea of *national efficiency* in the drive to mental and physical fitness, rooted in drill and discipline. 'The very illiberality of drill and discipline reflected the attitudes of those concerned with youth to "freedom" (and therefore chaos)' (Blanch, 1979: 118). *Model authority* was the second pervasive idea. Within these organizations we find a highly organized system of authority by ranks and levels and it was seen by their proponents as providing a model for social organization and leadership. The last theme was the *enemy outside*.

At least young people knew what they were joining. What was expected of them was clear. While there was some resistance to things like drill, military manoeuvres and uniforms, members were attracted by sport, the band and the annual camp (Humphries, 1981: 134–5). Further, there were significant differences between the Boys' Brigades and the Scouts. From the outset the Scouts were independent of one particular religious organization (although they might be attached to a Church or Chapel), and they utilized a rather different concept of discipline (seen as an inner quality, rather than something that had to be externally drilled) (Jeffs, 1979: 7).

If the aim of organizations such as the Boys' Brigade was to reform the behaviour and attitudes of the working-class young, those that reformers saw as 'being at risk', then they also failed. First, the uniformed organizations were, and still are, predominantly pre-adolescent. Secondly, the majority of working-class young people were in effect excluded from such organizations either because of the membership fees and the cost of uniforms, or because it was alien to their culture. There are numerous reports of the abuse and scorn poured upon Scouts or Boys' Brigades when they paraded in working-class neighbourhoods. A sample of Boys' Brigade membership in the 1890s, taken from enrolment books, demonstrates that sons of skilled manual workers or those with fathers in 'white collar' occupations clearly prevail over a negligible number with unskilled or semi-skilled parents (Springhall, 1977: 25). Of the 11,000 Scouts in London in 1910, Baden Powell calculated that about one-half or more came from the lower-middle class and the 1921 Census indicates that the South had a significantly higher density of Scouts per thousand teenagers than the industrial North (Springhall, 1977: 127). Thirdly, there was resistance from a significant proportion of those who did join. Yet, to some extent, such youth movements did allow the assimilation of upper-working class and lower-middle class boys into the new social order. They:

> helped to absorb the upwardly aspiring into the ranks above them in the status hierarchy: by training boys to become accustomed to a new social identity with the minimum of disturbance to the class fabric of society. For the socially ambitious, hard working apprentice, a youth movement became an intermediary, providing a *rite de passage* between and within classes. (Springhall, 1977: 121)

Those young men who wanted to advance within the existing system were provided with a means of preparing themselves in a way acceptable to those who presided over entry into desired jobs and social organizations. Those who did not wish to advance on these terms could at least be offered some recreation in the hope of containment. However, work with girls and young women tended to emphasize a different type of 'getting on', and suggests there were serious limits to this process.

Ennobling their class

While club leaders and Guide leaders often asserted that their aim was to develop habits of self-reliance and independence in girls and young women, the way in which this was interpreted and the reality of the work, on the whole, suggests rather different concerns. For instance, Agnes Baden Powell argued that a movement like Guiding was needed among working-class girls – 'the girls of the factories and of the alleys of our great cities' – because they would otherwise escape from any kind of restraining adult influence once they had left elementary school (quoted by Dyhouse, 1981: 113). Thus Guiding, girls' clubs, Snowdrop Bands and the Girls' Friendly Society could be seen as attempting to fill a 'gap'. Such girls would otherwise be influenced by their working-class peers and relatives:

> Too much independence amongst young girls was a dangerous thing. It is significant that in most of the literature expounding the need for clubs and societies amongst adolescent girls, the working girl's independence is perceived as 'precocity'. Wage earning is believed to buy them a premature and socially undesirable independence. Further there is a strong assumption . . . that financial independence and sexual precocity go hand-in-hand. (Dyhouse, 1981: 113)

It was feared that the involvement of young women in the labour market and, consequently, their spending power, would tempt girls away from their allotted roles of wife and mother. If young women were 'upwardly aspiring', then what such organizations could provide them with was an experience in the 'womanly arts' so that they might influence their men:

> If we raise the work girl, if we can make her conscious of her own great responsibilities both towards God and man, if we can show her that there are other objects in her life besides that of her gaining her daily bread or getting as much amusement as possible out of her days, we shall then give her an influence over her sweetheart, her husband and her sons which will sensibly improve and raise her generation to be something

higher than mere hewers of wood and drawers of water. (Stanley, 1890: 4–5)

However, it was important that girls did not get above their station. There were definite limits to the *rite de passage*: 'we have not wished to take our girls out of their class, but we have wished to see them ennoble the class to which they belong' (Stanley, 1890: 48). The bourgeois improvers could only ever offer a limited path between classes for both young men and women. They believed in, and operated within a system which required a particular division of labour and which would have considerable difficulties in accommodating large numbers of young people wanting significant advancement. While the rhetoric of individual achievement came easy, it had to be contained within particular class, gender, racial and age structures: a woman's place was in the home; to be British was to be best; betters were to be honoured; and youth had to earn its advancement and wait its turn.

Bourgeois youth work

When commentators examine the development of youth work, they usually use organizations as the means of defining their field of study. Groupings that were short-lived or informal are ignored, as are political activities and approaches that led to forms not normally associated with youth work:

> Youth work thus came to be the voluntary effort of groups of people outside the class and the age-group in need. Other possible solutions were rejected. . . . Those who were taking action clearly wanted to achieve something which, they believed, only they were capable of providing. (Davies and Gibson, 1967: 31)

In fact, much early work was directed at young people in the same class as the providers. However, those institutions which have subsequently become identified with youth work were largely controlled by members of the middle class. They carried with them specific themes (particularly an attack on working-class cultures), developed forms which are recognizable in present-day practice, and sought to engage the services of particular 'types' of adult. In this respect they have much in common with the notions of rational recreation that formed the initial development of the working men's clubs.

We have attempted to place youth work in history, but that

history in turn needs to be set within the forms of relationship that
have developed over time within society. The very middle class
that has been so prominent in the accounts of the development of
youth work, was itself produced within a system which has
something of its own dynamic. Many of the concerns that were
expressed by the early middle-class sponsors of youth work could be
seen as reflecting requirements of the economic system. However,
the relationship between the needs of the economic system and the
provision that was the outcome of the sponsors efforts, is far from
simple or straightforward (Jeffs and Smith, 1988a: 83–9). Indeed, at
one level, many of the improvers' efforts were directed at the
containment and reformation of elements of the system. No doubt
these early workers and philanthropists were sincere in their belief
that they were acting in the best interests of the young – that the
values and institutions they saw threatened were for the good of all
rather than the benefit of the few. Their thinking was formed within
a particular class which in turn was both the creation and beneficiary
of capitalism. Similarly, the organizations that they initiated had to
act within that system and inevitably took on values and ways of
operating which made sense both of and within that system. In
particular, because youth organizations were, and still are, in the
market economy, they have to respond to its dynamics much like
commercial operations (Jeffs and Smith, 1988a: 88). Those
advocating rational recreation and improvement were competing
with strong commercial forms, in particular the public house and its
large-scale derivatives such as the music hall.

   Youth work may have arisen out of bourgeois concerns about the
behaviour, beliefs and fitness of working-class young people, but the
philanthropists' best efforts were often frustrated by young people
themselves. Thus, youth work cannot adequately be portrayed as
exhibiting a simple one-way imposition of middle-class values and
behaviours upon the working-class young. Here the work of
Gramsci (1971) and, in particular the notion of hegemony, is
important. Hegemony is the process by which the dominant class
reproduces its ascendancy through the use of ideological means. It is
a moment when one concept of reality is diffused throughout society
and informs 'taste, morality, customs, religious and political
principles, and all social relationships, particularly in their intellectual and moral connotations' (Williams, quoted in Morris, 1979: 58).
Although certain ways of thinking become embedded in day-to-day
living, control is never complete. All that can be achieved is a
temporary or moving equilibrium. Within the dominant class there
will be constant movement and realignment. Similarly, he argues,

the working class manifests a dual consciousness, holding two apparently contradictory or inconsistent sets of beliefs at the same time. This consciousness is in part determined by bourgeois ideology and in part is commonsense knowledge derived from people's everyday experience of the world (Gramsci, 1971: 323–33). Thus, different social groups relate differently to the 'dominant' ways of thinking. As a result, subordinate classes do not acquiesce passively to the attempts by the ruling class to win consent to their authority and to exercise cultural leadership.

Ideology is presented here as a relatively autonomous set of ideas and practices which cannot simply be reduced to an expression of class interests or economic structure. The ideological terrain is, thus, a complex of discourses. In that complex, the balance of forces are 'always in flux and the site of contestation over meanings' (Thompson, 1986: 48). As such ideology both limits and enables. We are constrained by the ideas that we have – they allow us a particular view of the world, one that is inevitably partial. On the other hand, ideology does provide us with ideas and the possibility for developing a view of the world that allows us to act:

> Within this perspective, ideology refers to the production, consumption, and representation of ideas and behaviour, which can either distort or illuminate the nature of reality. As a set of meanings and ideas, ideologies can either be coherent or contradictory; they can function within the spheres of both consciousness and unconsciousness; and finally, they can exist at the level of critical discourse as well as within the sphere of taken-for-granted lived experience and practical behaviour. (Giroux, 1983: 143)

Giroux goes on to say that ideology is something that we all participate in; yet we rarely understand the historical constraints that produce and limit the nature of that participation. Nor do we appreciate 'what the possibilities are for going beyond existing parameters of action to be able to think and act toward a qualitatively better existence' (Giroux, 1983: 145).

It has been argued that 'the dominated classes do *not* hold the dominant ideology, the dominant classes *do*' (Abercrombie and Turner, 1982: 406). To the extent that there is a dominant ideology, 'it is best seen as securing the coherence of the dominant class' (Abercrombie and Turner, 1982: 411). In this way the attempts by early youth workers to reshape working-class cultures in the image of bourgeois norms and values can be understood as acting to confirm and consolidate the beliefs of both those workers and their sponsors. Yet we should not pursue this line too far. It may be that subordinated groups do not take on a cohesive, dominant ideology which subjects them totally to the domination of the ruling class, but 'the ideologies of nationalism and individual achievement may inhibit and confuse the development of the counter ideology of the subordinate class' (Thompson, 1986: 48). These confusing bourgeois ideologies were central to many early youth workers' efforts. 'Getting on' and the chance to 'serve Queen and Country' also figured strongly in the motives of a substantial number of their young adherents.

The extent to which the development of any counter-ideology is arrested is dependent, in part, upon the ability of the subordinate class to resist encroachment. Resistance may occur through the development of divergent sub-cultures such as that of the street (Roberts, 1973) or the pub (Foster, 1977: 223) (see Chapter 2). It may be helped further by those elements of capital whose interests are not served by the dominant ideology, in this case publicans and the entrepreneurs involved in many of the 'hated' popular leisure forms. Thus, 'all social actors, no matter how lowly, have some degree of penetration of the social forms which oppress them' (Giddens, 1979: 72). Not only do people exhibit a dual consciousness and to some extent 'see-through' potentially oppressive forms, they may also distance themselves from them:

> Where partially closed, localized cultures become largely unavailable, as is increasingly the case within advanced capitalism, scepticism about 'official' views of society often is expressed in various forms of 'distancing' – and in humour. Wit is deflationary. Humour is used both socially to attack and to defend against the influence of outside forces that cannot otherwise be coped with. (Giddens, 1979: 72)

The resistance of working-class young people to the emerging forms of youth provision displays the power of divergent sub-cultures, a level of awareness or seeing-through the social forms that sought to oppress them, and the use of distancing mechanisms such as larking about, humour and ridicule. At one level the forms and means of resistance may have seemed trivial or childish, but they did act to restrict bourgeois penetration of working-class cultures. Young people's resistance and reinterpretations played an important role in the defining of youth work. However, there was a limit to this resistance. In the end working-class young people basically complied with the economic and political system. Later, they joined youth organizations on a massive scale. Such acquiescence did not finally occur because young people had been consciously manipulated and incorporated into some dominant way of thinking. As Marx asserted: 'the advance of capitalist production develops a working class which by education, tradition, habit, looks upon the conditions of that mode of production as self-evident laws of nature. . . . The dull compulsion of economic relations completes the subjection of the labourer to the capitalist (Marx, 1887: 737). In other words, people's convictions flow from the requirements of everyday living. They want to survive and enjoy themselves, but this entails money within a capitalist system – 'the cash nexus remains, therefore, a major means of social, economic and political control' (Bocock, 1986: 32).

In this way bourgeois youth work was formed. It aimed to assist with the maintenance and development of the social and economic order envisaged by key members of the middle class. Secondly, it adopted and confirmed distinctively bourgeois forms and values. These were often drawn from the experience of public schooling and military service or represented paradigms of middle-class leisure. The 'club', particular notions of service and leadership, organized games and *esprit de corps*, and ideas about suitable activities and behaviours for 'ladies', are examples of this. Indeed, the notion of adolescence as it was articulated can be seen to be largely a bourgeois construction. Thirdly, it acted to salve middle-class consciences by enabling them to feel they were doing something about the worst excesses of capitalism. The very fact that *they* were providing help, and others were defined as not, also allowed them to justify their pre-eminent position. It was both a way of confirming superiority and status and of receiving thanks and gratitude (Fraser, 1973). Lastly, this work provided a range of opportunities for 'meaningful' endeavour for those members of the middle class who were denied entry or were unable to enter both the labour market and the representative political arena. A new form of welfare provision had arrived, but it was not to have the field to itself.

Chapter 2

The Making of
Popular Youth Work

The scope and scale of popularly organized leisure activities for young people has always been substantial. For example, children and young people have engaged in highly institutionalized but often informal forms of self-organized amusement for centuries. Perhaps the most obvious and universal of these are the games of the street and field such as football and pitch and toss (Opie and Opie, 1969), or amusements such as skipping and gambling. Street groups in the late 1800s and early 1900s also had values of which bourgeois society knew little, as Roberts' description of his Salford upbringing shows:

> The group constituted an open air society, a communal gathering which had great importance socially, culturally and economically. By tradition, membership stood hedged round with restrictions, all unformulated: indeed all participants were hardly conscious of a bond. . . . School-boys, girls, women and married men kept their distance, the last, of course, having their rendezvous socially much superior in the tavern.
>
> During each nightly meeting the young worker, once fully integrated, listened, questioned, argued and received unawares an informal education. Here work-a-day life beyond his personal ken came up for scrutiny. . . . All this was bread and butter talk vital at times to the listener, talk that had an economic scope and a variety to be heard nowhere else. (Roberts, 1973: 156–7)

Other street activities such as the 'monkey parade' on weekend evenings were more deliberately mixed:

> Girls resort to Oldham Street on a Sunday night, in nearly as

large numbers as the boys. The [boys] exchange rough salutations with the girls, who seem in no way less vigorous than the boys themselves, and whose chief desire, one would think, was to pluck from the lads' button-holes, the flowers which many of them wear. (Russell, 1905: 30)

In addition to the street, there are also many examples of mutual aid, of how young people organized themselves. Early youth organizations were no exception in this respect. There were a number of instances where groups of young men (and young women) came together and attempted to find an adult leader so that they might become an official Scout pack (Springhall, 1977). The boys' club movement boasts the celebrated example of 'The Deadhouse', a group of young men who organized their own club in 1909, largely around football, in a disused mortuary in Cable Street, East London (Dawes, 1975: 93–4). Outside the formal youth organizations young people used other types of institution. One example is the formation in 1875 of the Great Wigstone Working Men's Club, Leicester, by 'a few youths of the village tired of being chased around by the village constable' (Taylor, 1972: 18):

> They even had to borrow the four shillings and sixpence to pay the bellmans fee when he went around announcing their first meeting. His cries fell on respondent ears, and these early club men were able to rent premises in the shape of 'an asylum house'. This was a humble home; 'The furniture consisted of two old forms, and the place was illuminated by lamps and candles'. The first beverage to be drunk in the club was tea.
>   The first member to arrive lit the fire and put the kettle on, and became the steward for the night. With too many stewards this did not pay. It was eventually decided to try a small barrel of beer. Success was immediate. (Taylor, 1972: 18)

Aside from what working-class young people organized for themselves, there was also a considerable tradition of working-class adult provision aimed at young people. Of central importance here was the Sunday School. By the mid-1800s it could be argued that there were two mutually exclusive groupings within the urban working class: the first and larger sub-culture revolved around the public house; the second, smaller grouping rejected pub society and took to the chapel or church and adult education:

> While the self-educators spoke the language of their betters, the mass took pride in an aggressively opaque dialect. And while the social life of the smaller group was spent almost

entirely within an intimidating complex of formal institutions, the free-and-easy friendly society remained the only – and exceptional – organizing element for the majority. (Foster, 1977: 223)

Conclusions such as this need treating with care. By this time many Sunday Schools had passed into the control of working people, although the membership of chapels would appear to have been drawn rather more from the skilled than the unskilled working class (McLeod, 1984: 24). Three-quarters of working-class children were attending such schools in 1851 (Laqueur, 1976: 44). This was popular provision on a massive scale.

Laqueur suggests that the key element in the success of Sunday Schools was that they provided the education and expressed the values that working-class parents wanted for their children. In particular, it was the transmission of the values of the 'respectable' working class or labour aristocracy that were stressed – self-discipline, industry, thrift, improvement, egalitarianism and communalism. Sunday Schools, when considered in this light, parallelled other working-class institutions such as Friendly Societies, trade unions and savings banks. They mirror the achievements of the supplementary schools organized within Afro-Caribbean communities in recent years (Stone, 1981: 184–90). Sunday Schools were used not simply to improve literacy and religious knowledge, but also, arguably, to enhance the culture of working-class life.

However, the view that Sunday Schools were the actual creation of a working-class culture of respectability and self-reliance has been questioned. Dick (1980) claimed that Sunday Schools have to be seen as essentially middle-class conservative institutions directed at the improvement of working-class young people from above. Thompson argued that they helped contribute to the political defeats of working-class radicalism (1968: 411–40), although other writers have advanced the counter-argument that the Chapels and Sunday Schools were actually an integral part of the same movement (Hobsbawm, 1968). If we take the line of analysis developed at the end of Chapter 1, then it certainly can be argued that while the smaller sub-culture took on some bourgeois forms these may well have been re-made and reinterpreted and actually used against their 'betters'. Much seems to turn round the notion of 'respectability' and the extent to which it was reinterpreted within a working-class culture. We might, like Bailey, approach respectability as a role rather than as an ideology or a uniform life-style. Then:

the nature of class relations in leisure takes on a new light. Thus working class membership of church football teams can be seen as a purely instrumental attachment, calculated to extract certain benefits. . . . In this case working class behaviour which might have appeared as deferential from above, functioned as a kind of exploitation in reverse for its actors, who assumed respectability to meet the role demands of their class superiors. (Bailey, 1987: 185)

Whether such respectability was instrumental or distinctively working class or bourgeois, there can be no denying the scale and importance of these institutions in the lives of young people. Nor can the major role played in them by working-class people be neglected.

Aside from the educational contribution of Sunday Schools, Churches and Chapels also provided a forum for leisure. Services and associated activities had the special advantage of being one of the few organized and 'respectable' social occasions where sex segregation was not imposed. By the 1890s Joseph Lawson was able to write: .

Chapels are now more inviting – have better music – service of song – which cannot help being attractive to the young as well as beneficial to all. They have sewing classes, bazaars, concerts, and the drama; cricket and football clubs, and harriers; societies for mutual improvement and excursions to the seaside. (quoted in Cunningham, 1980: 181)

Such mutual aid provision has come to assume crucial importance in our experience of leisure, yet remarkably little is known about its history and nature (Bishop and Hoggett, 1986: 2).

By and large, commentators have also excluded consideration of the contribution of political movements to the education of young people. Some late nineteenth-century socialist organizations made specific provision for young people. The Clarion Scouts, started by Robert Blatchford in 1894 as groupings of young socialist pioneers, claimed by 1896 to have 120 clubs with 7000 members. Clarion Youth Houses were set up, forerunners of the Youth Hostels, and Clarion Scouts carried the socialist message to villages and towns on bicycles (Simon, 1965: 38). As with the religious Sunday School movement, however, there is some debate as to the class nature of the Clarion Clubs and Scouts, with the suggestion that membership was predominantly lower-middle class. Both Chartist and Owenite socialists had established Sunday Schools for children, but which had died out in the late 1840s. This tradition was revived in the 1880s and 1890s, and by 1910 when a national union was formed, around 100 schools were operating and were attended by nearly 5000 children and over 1000 adults (Simon, 1965: 48–52). A number of local cooperative societies ran youth sections, although these were often directed towards social and recreational ends. However, such examples exhibit a degree of age segregation which was unusual within the socialist and labour movement at that time.

For the most part these forms of young people's organizations did not have the degree of formality or structure that the middle-class sponsors of youth work would have recognized as their own. They did not conform to the paradigms of the 'youth organization' that existed. Nor were there the 'adults of good example' or 'ladies of culture' (presumably meaning subscribing to similar values and behaviours as the middle-class sponsors) except, perhaps, in the case of some of the Sunday Schools. Nor did they, for the most part, exhibit the qualities associated with the new 'science of charity', so powerfully extolled by organizations such as the Charity Organization Society (COS). Indeed, the working men's clubs and the Clarion Scouts at times sought to confront the dominance of the middle class. The nature of what these organizations offered was essentially different: it was not 'improvement' that they promised, in the sense of entry to the middle class or the assumption of bourgeois attitudes and behaviours, rather, by the late 1880s, they sought to advance the interests of the working class as a whole. In other words, their vision was essentially collectivist, whereas that of the middle-class providers of youth work was largely individualistic. Even much Sunday School activity stressed the importance of mutual aid and equality. However, a number of these organizations did share elements of bourgeois provision, such as the use of the club and the provision of educational opportunities: in most we do see social activities, although they were probably understood in a different way.

The bulk of those involved in the working-class forms described would not have thought of labelling their endeavours as youth work. The conceptualization of youth work around a supposed generational need or difference, and its underpinning by the notion of adolescence, would not have accorded with the experience of those engaged in working-class politics. The idea of adolescence was culturally bound and, far from accepting a youth–adult dichotomy, such activists 'emphasized precisely those outcomes which philanthropic youth work was seeking to prevent: a working-class solidarity nurtured in part by the [political] "corruption" of the young by their elders' (Davies, 1986: 95). Further, the main focus of the philanthropists' attentions, leisure, was not accorded much importance in male working-class political organizations. Compared with the workplace or the struggle to achieve reasonable educational opportunities for the working class, leisure appeared a secondary concern. Finally, many of the concerns and forms of bourgeois youth work did not resonate with the experiences of the working-class organizers. But much was to change.

Emerging patterns of youth work

Faced with their seeming inability to turn the advancing tide of mass commercial leisure and the growth of other forms of socializing provision, such as schooling and the mass media, many improvers began to reassess their interventions. At the same time, the continuing development of community-based forms of working-class organization, e.g. the Chapel and the tenants and community association, and the emergence of state intervention, and hence paid part-time youth work, heralded the conscious adoption of the epithet 'youth work' by those other than the bourgeois improvers. The pivotal period in this respect was the 1930s and 1940s.

During this period there was a substantial increase in young people's involvement in the newly emerging mass leisure industries. In particular, dancing and the cinema (Wild, 1979) excited considerable comment about their impact on the young, especially concerning their sexual morality. By the 1930s, 40 per cent of the population went to the cinema at least once a week. Two things are worthy of note here: first, the development of the cinema and dance hall expressed the changing relationships between the sexes, with a far higher degree of 'mixing'. Secondly, the cinema was one of the first mass leisure forms to appeal to, and come to be designed for, the leisure needs of women (Clarke and Critcher, 1985: 73). Other leisure forms also continued to evolve. Excursions and holidays developed under the impact of the growth of holiday pay, and mass-spectator sports such as football were regularly attracting large crowds.

At the same time home-based entertainment became more sophisticated and there were enhanced possibilities for it. Family size had declined and the housing conditions of many had improved. Generally, these factors combined to make the home a less crowded and more pleasant place to spend time in. In addition to the development of various card and board games, radio was introduced, and the ownership of luxury goods such as gramophones greatly increased. The number of radio licences increased from under 30 000 in 1922 to over 9.5 million by 1939. Other domestic hobbies that developed included model making, radio construction and model railways. Crucially, such hobbies also provided a focus for the development of enthusiast groups. These communal leisure groups provided a fairly unique opportunity for people to come together to produce something outside the usual confines of the market economy, primarily for consumption by themselves or their friends and neighbours (Bishop and Hoggett, 1986: 40).

These developments reflected a high degree of segregation, specialization and institutionalization. First, the growth of holidays away from home and the movement of housing away from industry enhanced the separation of work and leisure. Further, while the dance hall may have been mixed, gender still remained a powerful means of segregating leisure activities, as did class and region. Secondly, 'leisure institutions were increasingly aimed at attracting discrete bodies of leisure consumers rather than the public in general' (Clarke and Critcher, 1985: 78). In other words the market had become segmented. Finally, the new leisure industries depended upon small returns from a large number of users, and this confirmed the continuing institutionalization of leisure. Thus, the cinema, football grounds, dance halls, gaming establishments and the sale of many consumer products such as radios all relied upon this premise and, as a consequence, required large-scale organization and a customer–provider relationship. It is against these movements in leisure and the way in which they express the deeper workings of the economy and of the social structure, that the expansion of youth work that happened at this time has to be considered.

A number of important new actors entered the youth work stage. Of great significance was the development of community centres under the encouragement of the National Council for Social Service. These centres set out to integrate youth and adult provision in one unit, and the apparent success of the initiative 'led to the inclusion of Clause 80 in the 1936 Housing Act which conferred upon housing authorities the powers to enable them to make funds available for the construction and maintenance of community centres and recreation grounds for their tenants' (Jeffs, 1979: 13). Although many of the new community associations made only limited space available for young people, their growth, and that of village halls, did make a net addition to provision and to the youth work labour force (Rooff, 1935: 88; Morgan, 1939: 377). The harnessing of local enthusiasm was not without its problems though: 'One of the great difficulties . . . is to combine the initiative and independence of the neighbourhood group with the need for experienced leadership and specialist teachers in the organization of clubs for boys and girls' (Rooff, 1935).

The NCSS was also active in making monies available for the establishment of unemployment centres during the inter-war years. In part, this resulted from a desire to counter the efforts of the National Unemployed Workers Movement. A number of these Occupational Centres or Community Service Clubs sought to attract the young unemployed, but were largely unsuccessful. One survey found that the 'absence of democratic control provided the ground for the most serious of the criticisms offered by young men on the conduct of the Centres', and that the programmes offered were staid and unimaginative (Cameron *et al.*, quoted in Jeffs, 1979: 14).

To concerns about 'new' communities and unemployment were added worries about black children and young people. In those areas where there were black communities there is evidence of bourgeois intervention. For example, a 'liberal and white paternalistic organization' (Law, 1981: 31) known as the Association for the Welfare of Half Caste Children was set up in Liverpool in 1929. One report it sponsored in 1930 concluded that the problem of unemployment and destitute youth could be solved, not by tackling the problem of white racism in employment, but by 'replacing all black firemen by white on British ships coming to Liverpool' (Law, 1981): a conclusion hardly welcomed in the black community.

Black political and social organization continued to develop. Again in Liverpool, a number of social clubs and organizations were formed such as the Ethiopia Hall, which provided protective shelter during the racist riots of 1919 (Fryer, 1984: 301–302). In East London, Pastor Kamal Chunchie set up the Coloured Mens Institute in Canning Town in 1926. Significantly, this organization placed an emphasis on the needs of black children and young people, commissioning a special report in the early 1930s and providing activities for them including day trips to Southend (Widdowson, 1986). Chunchie was also involved in the League of Coloured Peoples, founded in 1931 in order to combat, among other things, the colour bar. It was described as a 'social club, housing bureau, pressure group and employment agency', in short 'Humanitarianism, Pan-African Style' (Drake, quoted in Fryer, 1984: 328). With a membership largely centred in Cardiff, Liverpool and London, it also organized activities for children and young people. Moody, one of its founders and its President until 1947, was anxious about the welfare of 'coloured' children and young people. On their prospects for jobs:

he felt it was a well-known fact that no black boy or girl could procure a job in any office no matter how qualified. No engineering works was willing to employ them, and apart from shipping they had no outlet. . . . Unfortunately, Moody's attention was on the individual rather than the system which produced and showed every sign of prolonging this tragedy. (Ramdin, 1987: 114)

Moody expended some effort in correspondence with various local authorities on these young people's behalf and held discussions with officers of the Juvenile Employment Bureaux.

As might be expected from the earlier account of Sunday Schools, churches were large-scale and diverse providers of leisure and educational opportunities for young people. Provision included sports clubs, dramatic clubs and guilds and fellowships for the older age ranges. As Garrett (1986) later found in her survey of youth provision in Croydon in the mid-1980s, many churches (and in particular, in Garrett's research, black churches) had been under-taking activities which were hidden from general surveys of welfare provision. When these were brought into contact with self-conscious youth work organizations they were liable to relabel their activities. Thus, with the development of uniformed work and the links made with national organizations such as the Girls' Friendly Society, the YWCA and the National Council of Girls' Clubs, such work was increasingly described as youth work.

The membership of some of the uniformed church organizations reached their peak during this period, with the Boys Brigade having 96 000 UK members in 1934, although these numbers dropped significantly with the outbreak of war. In contrast, membership of the Girls' Friendly Society declined and, it is apparent that during the 1930s, the churches and many youth organizations recognized the shifts occurring within the leisure market and felt some need to respond. Perhaps the most substantial changes occurred in the decision of many clubs and fellowships to be 'mixed' and to adopt a more directly social or recreational programme. In general, such clubs were rather more welcomed by the girls' club movement than the boys' club movement. The case for mixing was advanced on both educational and pragmatic grounds. The separation of the sexes was seen by the proponents of mixing as unnatural, the creation of an artificial barrier. In addition, they feared that they would be unable to carry on with youth work on any substantial scale in the long term unless mixing was introduced in some way, simply because this was what was demanded by the young. Other factors contributed to this movement including the organizational difficulties of running twin clubs with separate girls' and boys' activities on different nights.

Significantly, a tradition emerged within church work of clubs and fellowships 'usually organised and planned by the Young Peoples' Committee' (Rooff, 1935: 29). However, Rooff identifies two main areas of concern in church-associated work – the first being difficulties with premises and the second the danger of sectionalism:

> Many are able to do the valuable work amongst the small groups attached to them which is sometimes difficult of attainment in the larger club. On the other hand, there is the danger of too great concentration on their own small units, and a narrow loyalty may lead to a refusal to co-operate in larger issues of the neighbourhood. (Rooff, 1935: 35)

Jewish youth workers also continued to adapt and in particular had to take account of social mobility. The suburban clubs which opened in London in the 1930s 'brought about a major reappraisal of the pattern and character of Jewish youth work' (Bunt, 1975: 27).

School-based youth work made its appearance, perhaps the best known example being the first Cambridge Village College at Sawston, opened by Henry Morris in 1928. A number of LEAs were encouraging the development of Old Scholars' Clubs, while others were turning an official blind eye. Their programmes are reminiscent of those of the Chapel and Sunday School at the end of the nineteenth century:

> A diversity of tastes and needs is catered for, and winter activities include physical training, country dancing, lectures, reading circles, craft work and dramatic performances. In summer, contact is maintained with the old scholars by means of rambles, cycling and other forms of outdoor sport. (Rooff, 1935: 43)

In London in 1935 there were some 250 of these clubs meeting generally once a week in school premises provided free of charge by the London County Council.

The entry of the state into the youth work arena was originally signalled in the report of the Russell Committee at the end of the First World War which advocated the setting up of local juvenile organizations' committees to coordinate the provision of facilities for young people (Jeffs, 1979: 11–12). The committee also recommended that LEAs should have the power to give financial support to such committees and to certain voluntary organizations. Fisher, in his Education Act (1918), drew on the committee's recommendations and gave LEAs the powers to spend money on facilities for physical training, organized games, holiday camps and for the social training of young people in the evening, which 'in essence meant that they could if they so desired make grants available to youth clubs and groups' (Jeffs, 1979: 12). Little money was in fact made available until the mid-1930s, when grants were made to voluntary organizations in depressed areas by the Special Areas Commissioner and to the YMCA for outdoor pursuits in junior transfer centres by the Ministry of Labour. The Physical Training and Recreation Act (1937) conferred permissive powers on LEAs to make provision for physical training instruction and recreational facilities for the 14–20 age group. Further action had to wait for the war.

The Youth Service and wartime disruption

At the beginning of the Second World War there was mass transportation to the countryside in expectation of bombing and disruption. This, combined with the break-up of families through mobilization, the re-entry of married women into the labour market (and hence the need for provision for children), and other changes occasioned by wartime conditions, led to an immediate review of a number of welfare services by the government departments concerned. When the invasion did not immediately materialize a good proportion of the evacuees returned to the cities:

> The absence of one or both parents, abrupt changes of employment, long dark evenings and inadequate facilities for recreation combined to produce an urgent need for action. . . .
> The existing youth organizations had been hit by the call-up of youth leaders and workers, by the drastic commandeering of premises, by the running down of the income of the voluntary organizations and by the wholesale closure of youth clubs as an air raid precaution in evacuation areas. (Gosden, 1976: 211–12)

At the same time there was a substantial rise in juvenile delinquency, most commonly taking the form of larceny. The government could not remain idle. Circular 1486, *In the Service of Youth* (Board of Education, 1939), heralded the 'fourth province' of the education service after primary, secondary and adult education. The Circular talked of the neglect that the 14–20 age group had suffered in its physical and social development. It also noted the social problems of young people that had arisen during the First

World War. LEAs were urged to constitute Youth Committees, whose first duty was to formulate an ordered policy 'which shall provide for meeting the most immediate needs and which shall indicate the lines on which a real advance can be made under more favourable conditions' (Board of Education, 1939: 2). This was quickly followed by Circular 1516, *The Challenge of Youth* (Board of Education, 1940: 2), which laid down that LEAs 'are to take the initiative in their local areas; provide the machinery for local cooperation; encourage existing organizations to extend their work; and fill the gaps not covered by such organization'. The people charged with this task were to be Youth Officers and Organizers.

A year later it seemed as if the State was about to take a further step – compelling young people to belong to youth organizations. This was to be the first stage in the introduction of pre-military training. However, the practical and ideological questions were such that, the resulting Circular 1577 (Board of Education, 1941) simply required all young people aged 16 and 17 to register with their LEA. Young people were also to be interviewed and advised as to how they might spend their leisure time and of the local opportunities for them to give voluntary help to the war effort. This was usually done under the auspices of local youth committees. At first there was an attendance rate nationally of around 70 per cent. But as people began to realize the interview was not compulsory, the rate dropped, and the system was gradually dismantled as pressure for a pre-military training scheme disappeared.

One of the key responses made by the LCC and a number of LEAs, particularly in the north of England, was to open civic youth clubs or recreation centres, often in school buildings. Indeed, by the end of the war, Barnes reported that in his local survey, nearly three-quarters of all youth groups met in schools or in church halls (1945: 108). The new civic or recreational youth centres were frequently open on three or more nights in the week. In these centres:

> boys and girls not attached to any organization could go in an emergency, and these rapidly became of use during the blackout hours of the winter evenings. Although these youth centres were started to meet an emergency and on a temporary basis, numbers of boys and girls, hitherto untouched by any social organization, have joined these and similar centres and in many cases they have developed into permanent clubs. (National Council of Girls' Clubs 1940, quoted in Bunt and Gargrave, 1980: 111)

As Brew reports, these clubs also attracted some harsh criticism for 'giving their members no definite instruction, for concentrating on ballroom dancing, for being entirely secular, and for being mixed' (1943: 56). One of the innovations much talked about was the so-called 'In and Out Club' which did not require formal membership and young people could use as they wish. The *Times Educational Supplement* (29 June 1940: 255), following the publication of Circular 1516, hoped that any further financial support for the LCC's 'deplorable recreation centres' would be ruled out. Much of the other opposition to the new developments came from existing youth organizations, concerned about 'possible competition for membership from new organizations apparently favoured and backed by the government' (Gosden, 1976: 217).

Many of the new 'open clubs' were staffed by part-time paid workers, large numbers of whom had no previous experience of youth work. They came without many of the preconceptions of those in the older youth movements and tended to design programmes to attract, rather than to 'improve', young people. One of the major concerns was to keep young people's morale up as well as providing activities for them in safety. The shortage of staff and the development of members' committees were also contributory factors:

> Drama, arts, crafts, games and physical recreation were popular and were introduced with the idea that the senior members would return to their clubs, and build up the numbers necessary to justify the appointment of an Instructor, appointed and paid by the Local Education Authority. (Evans, 1965: 29)

Figures concerning the fitness of conscripts to the armed forces show why there was not a major moral panic concerning young men's ability to 'contribute to the war effort'. During the period of the War, 70 per cent of conscripts were found to be fully fit, compared with 36 per cent during the second half of the First World War (Rowntree, 1941). However, there was still an emphasis upon fitness in a number of official pronouncements and this led the Youth Committee of the Commission of Churches to send a deputation to complain of this emphasis and the relative neglect of religion in Circular 1516 (Gosden, 1976: 216).

The massive expansion of youth clubs was not restricted to urban areas. The impact of the evacuation of large numbers of school children and the billeting of troops in rural areas led to an expansion of rural provision. This was scarcely halted by the return of many of the evacuees to the urban areas. In general, rural provision took a similar form to that in the cities in that it adopted a broadly social model, although provision was often only on one night a week. In one very small rural area, where in June 1940 there were no clubs, there were 25 three years later (National Association of Girls' Clubs Annual Report, 1943).

Another feature of 'modern' youth work attracted attention at this time, i.e. detached work. Many policy documents expressed concern about the large numbers of young people who were not attached to youth organizations. One response was an attempt to encourage membership through registration, while another was to go to the places where young people were and to work with them there. Within youth work there has been a tradition, certainly dating back to Stanley (1878) and before, of going out onto the streets in order to find young people with the general intention of enrolling them in a youth organization. However, with large numbers of young people spending time in shelters, and with the closure of a number of traditional youth facilities, there was a demand for alternative forms of working. Paneth (1944) provides an account of one such project and poses a series of questions that remain fundamental to the work:

> Have we been intruders, disturbing an otherwise happy community, and is it only the bourgeois in us, coming face to face with his opponents, who minds and wants to change them because he feels threatened? Or *do* they need help from outside? (Paneth, 1944: 121)

Here we see a form of self-questioning that would have been unthinkable to the early exponents of youth work. Beyond that there had been a substantial shift in youth work's overall character, particularly with the emphasis on programmes that would attract young people. Most, if not all the changes, were prefigured in the 1930s with wartime conditions accelerating their adoption. The extent of the changes can be gauged by the second report of the National Youth Advisory Council, which argued that four characteristics distinguished the Youth Service's contribution from those of other agencies.

The purpose of the Youth Service is to promote and provide the opportunity for participating in activities:

1 which are carried on in a community different in its nature from school or work;
2 which are voluntarily undertaken;
3 which are complementary to other activities;

4 to which the approach is from the standpoint of recreation. (Ministry of Education, 1945: 7–8)

The Report unequivocally stated that 'the purpose of activities undertaken within the Youth Service should be recreation and enjoyment' (Ministry of Education, 1945: 9). The contrast with the rhetoric of character-building and child-saving could not be starker. Significantly, there was rather more emphasis on collectivities and 'collective self discipline'. 'Whatever the activity, and whatever the precise *motif*, the lessons to be learned are the same, cooperation, tolerance, free decision and joint responsibility' (Ministry of Education, 1945: 10): a conclusion which echoes a proposal to the Board of Education by the London Probation Service in 1940, where clubs in shelters were proposed in order to evoke the public spirit lacking in 'this individualistic society' (quoted in Gosden, 1976: 222). The report met with a less than adoring response in a number of youth organizations, but it undoubtedly articulated a mood and direction which was prevalent in a large swathe of the new provision. Although at the end of the war youth work had suffered severely from cuts in grant aid from central government funds and the loss of a substantial number of leaders as they returned to 'normal' activities, many of the mixed 'social' clubs remained.

The new youth workers

The entry of schooling, community associations and the State into youth work has been associated with a watershed in the class location and organization of those directly sponsoring and undertaking youth work. The relative proportion of workers from middle-class backgrounds decreased: 'Endowed with greater wealth and leisure than ever before, the groups from which the caretaker elites had once been recruited began to withdraw into a more self-centred private existence' (Gillis, 1974: 200). Part of the reason for this may have been the increasing proportion of married women who were working. As Percival noted, the feeling of *noblesse oblige* 'continued to produce social volunteers so long as there was a leisured class which had been given time to acquire this feeling' (1951: 211). However, it was not simply a matter of the middle classes withdrawing from such work, it was also that 'the supply of those who are willing to devote themselves to this arduous service has not expanded proportionately to the demand' (Morgan, 1939: 399). In other words, there was a substantial increase in the numbers of clubs and units during this period and in the numbers of young people

attending them. Significantly, these groups were largely accommodated within organizations which were largely devoted to other
activities, be they schooling, worship or broad community
provision. They were unlike the traditional bourgeois paradigms of
youth provision, represented by the free-standing boys' club, the
uniformed organization, or the improving group such as the Girls'
Friendly Society.

The large-scale entry of the State is of central importance. As the
State increasingly took over functions necessary for the maintenance
and reproduction of labour power, youth work became viewed as a
possible, but limited, site for intervention. At the same time, with
the extension of secondary education and mass communications
reinforcing popular commitment to national norms and values,
alternative forms of affirming social and political responsibility were
readily available. Thus, the formal entry of the State must be seen in
the peculiar circumstances of the period. Youth work was perceived
as having some potential to contribute to the productive and fighting
effort by providing enhanced opportunities for leisure and by
channelling people into voluntary productive activities via projects
such as the youth squads. Crucially, the entry of the State was also to
provide a generalized demonstration of the commitment and
concern of the State towards helping and supporting young people
en masse and individually (Jeffs and Smith, 1988a: 37–40). This was
further reinforced by claiming a special concern for those young
people with 'special needs':

> Consequently, youth movements made less of an appeal to the
> upwardly mobile than before, while their role as agencies of
> social management became increasingly superfluous. Only the
> lower-middle classes, with their status anxieties, patriotism,
> and political assertiveness, continued during the interwar
> period to provide leaders with enthusiasm at a local level.
> (Springhall, 1977: 124)

This latter grouping provided many leaders and workers. When
Rooff's (1935) survey on girls' clubs is analysed, a significant number
of the leaders were drawn from church congregations, with
relatively few from among teachers and 'leisured women', although
this appeared to vary from region to region. Significant occupational groupings included office workers and business women,
students, Church Army sisters and nuns and welfare workers in
factory clubs. The other major grouping were senior club members.
Others were restricted by material circumstances:

> Local efforts to support clubs are necessarily limited, since the

incomes of the residents leave little in excess of household needs. Moreover, the question of leadership is a vexed problem, since most of the women in the area have had neither the opportunities to develop wider interests nor the time to devote to running clubs etc. for young people. (Rooff, 1935: 71)

Morgan reported that 'leaders are being recruited from every walk of life', and that in the Special Areas, 'many unemployed men are assisting the work (1939: 401), a situation which was clearly not to his élitist tastes:

A large and increasing number of club leaders are men who have not had the advantages of an extended and liberal education. . . . The less well-educated leader can manage a sports institution or shelter from the street where boys can play billiards, and he may give them much of value for the formation of character; he may be a most valuable helper, but he is incapable of inspiring and organising a real club as of being headmaster of a school. (Morgan, 1939: 402)

During the expansion of youth work at the beginning of the war, a large number of people from local neighbourhood organizations as well as a substantial number of teachers were involved in the provision of youth work: a position further encouraged in some areas by payment. There was 'little or no difficulty in recruiting leaders and helpers. The need to assist young people under wartime conditions appealed to many as an urgent form of community service' (Evans, 1965: 23).

The professional youth worker and officer had also arrived, although some full-time workers had been employed previously in voluntary organizations. Now full-time officers and organizers were required to carry out the duties laid upon LEAs and it was argued that 'club service is elaborate and exacting, and many clubs have reached a stage of development where the regular presence of the leader is essential and it is not practicable to secure this on a voluntary basis on the scale which the movement now demands' (Morgan, 1939: 403). In 1944 the McNair Report advocated the training of professional workers, who would be drawn from the widest possible range of backgrounds (Board of Education, 1944). Employment in industry or commerce was considered a prerequisite for entry and, therefore, maturity in terms of years was given a high priority. Partly in order to attract such candidates, McNair argued for an independent training scheme: 'We do not think that training for youth leadership should be attempted within the course designed to train teachers and other kinds of social worker' (Board of Education, 1944: 104). The training scheme was to be of three years duration and located within the university sector of HE. The later Jackson Committee advocated a rather different course of action, recommending that teachers should be the main source of recruitment (Ministry of Education, 1949), a position which has subsequently been realized (Kuper, 1985).

Young people played a significant role in the organization of clubs and this was reflected in contemporary reports and policy statements (Evans, 1965: 18). During the Secord World War, this trend appears to have been strengthened by the shortage of adult leaders and the numbers of senior members who were called up. Further, in the hot-house atmosphere of war, the club was seen as important in the training of citizenship, 'as a little commonwealth, having its place in a democracy' (Edwards-Rees, 1943: 84). Overall, it would appear that much greater responsibility for the running of clubs was given to senior members and many came to resemble mutual aid institutions, although there was some problems of turnover in the special conditions of the war. A range of senior member training schemes were set up at local, regional and national levels. At the same time there was also 'the spontaneous desire of young people who had left school but were too young for the Services to do some form of national work' (Gosden, 1976: 223). Considerable numbers of young people joined local youth service squads which again were often self-organized.

Changing membership

Along with these significant shifts in the backgrounds and concerns of those running youth work provision, there was a major expansion and movement in membership. Surveying the developments during the war in one area, Barnes comments;

> In October 1944 there were some 900 youth groups known to the LEAs in our region, with a total membership of from 22 000 to 24 000. The membership fluctuates seasonally within fairly wide limits. But it is safe to say that, amongst the 14–18 age-group, 40 to 50 per cent of the girls and 50 to 60 per cent of the boys are in 1944–5 attached to some group. This represents a threefold expansion since 1939. (Barnes, 1945: 106)

Making sense of attendance figures and of the various surveys of leisure habits undertaken at this time is a task fraught with difficulties. When Jeffs examined the raw data on group membership collected by Morgan in 1938, he found that the figures gave an overall affiliation rate of 15.8 per cent, which does not seem out of line with what Barnes suggests. By late 1940, Board of Education figures suggest a total membership of youth organizations of 750 000 or around 25 per cent of 14–18 year olds (Gosden, 1976: 219). The registration scheme appears to have further increased the membership of youth organizations, initially by around 15–20 per cent, although such figures are open to dispute (Gosden, 1976: 228).

Having reached a peak during the war, by the late 1940s the overall number of young people taking part in Youth Service activities showed a decline. This was partly due to falling birth rates, but also to the shortage of experienced leaders, the withdrawal of funding and the growing opposition from groups such as teachers who felt that youth work was diverting young people from their educational endeavours. There was also a less intense sense of purpose in such activities following the cessation of hostilities. However, national surveys of the uses of leisure among secondary school children and out-of-school youth, plus many local surveys, still demonstrated a significantly higher usage than prior to the war. For instance, the Youth Service in the early 1950s was able to recruit around 75 per cent of school-age youth at some point. As before, when young people left school they usually stopped attending youth provision. Investigators also discovered a trend, that as teenagers aged, so they grew away from the older uniformed organizations towards membership of social clubs, whether run by local authorities or churches (Roberts, 1983: 14–15). When these figures are compared with later surveys a degree of stability appears. For instance, a survey published in 1972 showed that while around 26 per cent of 14–20 year olds belonged to a club at the time of the survey, 65 per cent belonged to some organized group (although often outside the Youth Service) and 93 per cent had belonged to an organized group at some time (Bone and Ross, 1972).

A question that these early figures leave open concerns the class location of users. A reasonable assumption is that in both absolute and relative terms, the working-class membership of youth organizations increased during this period. The bulk of this increase would appear to reside in the expansion of open youth work. However, while there was a shift towards working-class usage, grammar-school pupils were still more likely to attend youth clubs and youth organizations than were those attending secondary modern schools (Ward, 1948). Certainly by the early 1980s, open youth work displayed a different distinctive pattern:

Usage of youth clubs was age, sex and class determined to a considerable degree. Significantly more C2DEs (67%) had ever attended a youth club than ABC1s (57%) and this was reflected in the current usage pattern; . . . of the 14 to 16 year old 'teenagers' nearly 2 in 5 (38%) were currently going to a youth club compared with less than 1 in 5 (19%) of the over 16s; around one third (32%) of the boys attended a youth club compared with just over one quarter (26%) of the girls. (DES, 1983b: 36)

Their image, the report concluded, was 'essentially young, male and C2DE' (DES 1983b: 44). The new provision, while titled 'mixed', was weighted towards young men. For example, of those currently attending youth clubs in the above survey just 46 per cent were female (DES, 1983b: 37) and there is considerable evidence that this figure overstates their usage. Data collected by ILEA shows that it is only in the under-12 age ranges that girls constitute such a proportion of membership; in the crucial 14–15 age ranges they comprise 37 per cent of membership and in the 16–18 range 30.6 per cent (ILEA, 1984: 8). Further, such statistics as we possess, 'while appearing to confirm the hypothesis that the rate of girls' participation in the Youth Service is less than that for boys, and that it decreases with age, cannot be seen as reliable indicators of activity' (ILEA, 1984: 2). In other words, the position may be worse when actual usage is considered.

With the development of specific forms of black youth provision, often associated with black churches (Garrett, 1986), demographic movements (Ramdin, 1987: 253–4) and, arguably some shifts in cultural patterns of control of parents over their adolescent children, the usage of youth provision by black young people has substantially increased. In particular, Afro-Caribbeans are now twice as likely to attend youth clubs than are whites (DES, 1983b: 76). However, Asians were least likely of all to use youth provision with the exception of sports centres and school clubs, where, it is suggested, parental constraints do not operate as strongly (DES, 1983b: 36). Again, the emergence of unique forms of mutual aid provision via religious and cultural organizations and the various Asian youth movements has been of particular significance, and a great deal of provision remains 'hidden' from the usual surveys of welfare. While attendance figures for youth work provision may have improved, the extent to which such provision actually meets the expressed needs of black young people is limited (Williams, 1988).

Popular youth work

The expansion of youth organization membership, an apparent increase in the participation rates of working-class and black young people, the emphasis on self-organization, shifts in the class location of workers, the emergence of 'professionals', the entry of the State and the school, the significance of community organizations, and the general movement from notions of improvement to those of enjoyment, combine to make this a momentous period for youth work. But does this amount to the making of a *popular* youth work?

As Williams has noted, 'popular' was originally a legal and political term taken from *popularis*, meaning belonging to the people (1976: 198). Thus, popular culture could be understood as that made by people for themselves. In this sense, 'people's' youth work had arrived by the end of the Second World War. Programmes were adopted which contained cultural practices, such as mixing, dancing and informal discussion, which were associated in the minds of the providers with working-class leisure activities. The location of much provision within community-based organizations strengthens this view, as does the extent to which young people actually organized provision.

A competing understanding of 'popular' is 'well liked'. This contains 'a strong element of setting out to gain favour, with a sense of calculation' (Williams, 1976). According to this second meaning, popular culture has not been identified by *the people*, but by others. Often there is an accompanying judgement that popular forms are inferior, especially when compared with 'real' art or 'the novel'. Thus, when some of the developments in youth work are analysed in this way, they could again assume the label 'popular'. They display a number of the elements present in the development of mass entertainment. Even though this has been a time of mixed social provision, segregation, specialization and institutionalization still occurred and developed in a way parallel to other leisure industries (Clarke and Critcher, 1985: 78). Provision was specifically offered and designed that might appeal to a 'mass' market. The new 'low' popular forms could be compared unfavourably with 'real' youth work, which might be about improvement, leadership or spirituality.

From the foregoing it may be seen that there are two usages of the term 'popular'. However, this view has to be treated with some care, the distinctions and definitions are not that straightforward. All culture contains a moment of domination *and* the possibility of producing the ideological and material tools needed to begin to transform an oppressive social reality (Giroux, 1983: 226). Hence, popular culture is neither 'the site of the people's cultural deformation nor as that of their cultural self-affirmation . . . or of their self-making; rather it is . . . a force field of relations shaped, precisely, by these contradictory pressures and tendencies' (Bennett, 1986a: xiii). It is this force field within youth work which has produced the uncomfortable accommodations that go to make up popular practice and the way in which youth work is defined. The resistance of working-class young people to many bourgeois forms, the impact of commonsense economic imperatives, and the desire to rescue and improve the young are examples of these forces and have been represented here via the idea of a 'historic bargain' between workers, sponsors and young people – a bargain which is rarely made explicit:

> To put it crudely, people who support youth work by their money are seldom willing to support a venture which supplies nothing but what they like to call "mere amusement". . . . Therefore the unfortunate leader is too often in the unenviable position of being forced to embark on a programme which shall satisfy the desire for uplift demanded by the subscribers to the club, and at the same time to cater for the club member who is not ready for this uplift and resists it to the last gasp. It is this Puritanical conception that if people are enjoying themselves they are probably not learning anything which is at the root of much of the acknowledged dishonesty behind many annual reports. (Brew 1943: 49)

Significantly, stripped of the requirement to maintain morale following the end of the war, the language of official reports once again became peppered with references to character and to Christianity (see, e.g. King George's Jubilee Trust, 1951).

A further tendency in the use of 'popular' has been to equate implicitly 'the people' with the working class, and often the male working class at that. This, in turn, has often rested on the further assumption that 'the tensions and conflicts which are worked out and expressed in the sphere of popular culture are reducible to a single contradiction: that between working class culture and bourgeois ideology' (Bennett, 1986b: 15). This results in a failure to take account of the other 'multiple contradictions and struggles which traverse the class-related aspects of cultural struggle and deeply mark the face of popular culture' (Bennett, 1986b). These include the struggles of women against male domination and that against racism.

For these reasons it is not possible to allocate a fixed meaning to terms such as 'the people' or 'popular', rather they have to be viewed as contested and essentially political. It is in this way that we can talk of the making of popular youth work. Aspects of bourgeois youth work can be claimed as 'popular', as can certain commercial forms of provision such as the music hall. Nevertheless, bourgeois youth work may be contrasted with examples of activities which are characterized by face-to-face organizing relationships and which express their identity through forms which are seen as 'popular'. A significant number of the new 'open' clubs and groups were social, convivial, and had a symbiotic relationship with their members' cultures. Such organic youth work had an identity which lay with some notion of the 'popular'. While bourgeois youth work may use 'popular' forms, it appeals to a rather different set of ideas and practices when seeking to make sense of itself.

It would be nice to be able to call the non-bourgeois popular forms 'proletarian' in order to give symmetry to the model, but subsequent developments in youth work demonstrate the strength of Bennett's (1986b) argument. The most significant movements in what might be called oppositional and possibly anti-bourgeois practice in the 1970s and 1980s, have been found within consciously black or feminist practice. Located within social movements, portraying positive images, making explicit reference to ideology and culture, and linking the realms of personal and political experience, some of the practice generated has demonstrated how popular forms can be used in order to approach, understand and combat an oppressive social reality (M. Smith, 1987: 17–24). These cannot be seen as expressions of simple class-related struggles. Indeed, some of the work labelled feminist, for example, is also bourgeois. Further, it may also be that class analysis requires 'reconceptualization in the light of an extended exploration of race' (Gilroy, 1987: 223) and that we need to look at the ways in which experiences of gender and race are articulated within class relations.

Unlike that other middle-class-improving foray into working class leisure, the working men's club, young people have had to wait a long time to throw off bourgeois intervention. By 1886 the workers had gained control of that movement and it was able to 'bid a long farewell to all its great ones' (Hall, quoted in Simon, 1965: 73). The 1930s and 1940s mark something of a bourgeois farewell in youth work as popular forms of practice gained ascendancy. Even though some popular practice was simply the result of a growing bourgeois accommodation of working-class cultural forms, it still holds within it 'clusters of potential' (Yeo and Yeo, quoted in Bailey, 1987: 11). While bourgeois youth work can inhibit the development of an ideology and practice which serves the interests of subordinated groups, popular youth work at least furnishes possibilities for a counter-practice (see Chapter 8).

Chapter 3

Definition, Tradition and Change in Youth Work

Youth work is often portrayed and experienced as ever-changing, yet underlying this seeming movement are powerful continuities. Certain patterns of thinking and practice have existed over time and these can be recognized in apparently 'new ' work. For example, in the realm of black provision, supplementary schooling shares much with the earlier Sunday Schools; the stress on character and leadership in some approaches would be familiar to Baden Powell; and the consciously political connections made by some of the youth movements link with the early efforts of the Clarion Scouts and Woodcraft Folk. How is it then, that successive generations of youth workers and practitioners, faced with changing economic and social situations, have apparently adopted approaches that contain many elements in common with their predecessors' work?

When looking around for ways of describing or categorizing these apparent patterns in youth work, one typically comes up with 'either/or' distinctions. Examples of this form of distinction would be voluntary/statutory, full-time/part-time and detached/club-based. These may shed some light on the work but they can be seriously misleading and limiting (Hanmer, 1964). For instance, the detached/club-based distinction may tell us something about the initial institutional location of the client group, but beyond that we enter muddy waters. Club workers and detached workers can share the same conception of purpose, adopt the same means of intervention and work with the same target group. While there are differences arising from the relationship of the worker and young people to the setting in which they are operating, such a form of distinction requires serious qualification if it is to mean anything.

Another way of looking at youth work is to categorize its practice by the administrative or institutional base of the particular unit or project. Thus, youth work might be labelled as free-standing, school-based, church-based, local education authority, uniformed and so on (see e.g. Brew, 1943; Thomas and Perry, 1975; Garrett, 1986). The significance of breaking down youth work into these categories is that it can point to organizational structures and their associated ideologies. However, it may say very little about the work found in a specific setting, have little meaning to those who work in and use the provision, and it can render fundamental differences concerning the essential purposes of youth work unproblematic.

The major work of categorization in the last decade is that by Butters and Newell (1978). They suggested that, historically, there are three main perspectives in youth work. The first is *character building*, whose proponents sought to reduce what they saw as a major threat to the values and the society they believed in by the advance of the working class and, in particular, in the behaviour of young people. The thinking behind this approach was that young people could be integrated into society if they were exposed to adequate ideological training. 'If enough character is produced by education and youth work, the mature citizens that emerge will find a way to make institutions of the country run smoothly and humanely' (Butters and Newell, 1978: 41).

The second broad approach, *The Social Education Repertoire*, is presented as being significantly different from the character-building approach which preceded it. Between the two there is a 'critical break'. Within the repertoire, Butters and Newell suggest three main elements. The first, 'cultural adjustment', is symbolized by the Albemarle Report (HMSO, 1960) and portrays the main job of youth work as being to help young people to become 'healthy' adults rather than to alter society's institutions in order to encourage development. The youth work process is described as the 'non-directive enabling of individuals towards self-realization' (Butters and Newell, 1978: 39). The central concern of the second element, 'community development', is the lack of access of young people to the processes of decision making within the community. This expression, found in the Milson-Fairbairn Report (DES, 1969), although possessing many elements of cultural adjustment, particularly when describing the younger adolescent, did see community involvement as the key issue for the older age range. 'Institutional reform' is the third element and here the main process involves the mobilizing of individuals and groups to work for structural changes and the extension of rights. This approach, it was suggested, has been present spasmodically since the 1890s. While there may be differences between these elements, perhaps best illustrated by their perception of the status quo, it could be said that they share a number of qualities that make their incorporation into one overall approach possible. For example, they include the sharing of a respect for liberal humanism, i.e. the belief that intervention is justified if it helps people to live more happily with themselves, each other and society.

The last overall approach is labelled *self emancipation*. To reach this, another 'critical break' is required because, as Butters and Newell argue, the great majority of young people can only fulfil their potential if they join together in a struggle to overthrow the institutions and ideologies of the dominant classes. In this process, neither the 'harmony' nor the 'happiness' of all members of society can be guaranteed.

Butters and Newell's analysis was a welcome advance in the anti-intellectual climate of youth work but it was, nevertheless, deeply flawed. There is a tension in the writing between a desire to build from the extensive interviews they conducted with practitioners and trainers and a concern for academic legitimation. In the end we are left with something of an illusion – practitioners' views and perceptions are woven into a web that owes rather more to 'grand theory' than to their own concerns. Despite all of Butters and Newell's protestations the model is, in essence, 'top down'. Practitioners' and trainers' views are there as an illustration rather than the base for theory-making. Leigh and Smart put this slightly differently when they suggested that there is no substantial examination of the relationship between youth work practice and the ways that practitioners describe their work – the latter being variously and loosely termed theory, rhetoric or ideology (1985: 92). This leads on to what looks like a major misreading of what practitioners and trainers are saying and a focus on the welfaring, policing and schooling aspects of workers' practice rather than on those aspects directed toward peer-group support and enjoyment. As a consequence, Butter and Newell do not address in any substantial way the dominant forms of practice outside uniformed youth work. In particular, they do not explore in any depth the nature of practice which is here associated with popular youth work. The concern to build on grand theory also leads to the use of language and descriptions that, on the whole, stand only a slim chance of being recognized by practitioners and trainers. Finally, very little justification is given for the use of critical breaks between the social education repertoire and the other forms. Indeed, the Steering Group for this piece of research, questioned the placing of the breaks

(Butters and Newell, 1978: 52–3). Yet, what Butters and Newell do provide is a very necessary emphasis on the ideological and cultural nature of youth work and the extent to which this serves the interests of capital. They also give us a glimpse of the possible power of thinking about practice in a way that provides for the subtleties and complexities of everyday youth work, but as a way of naming the work, their analysis is lacking.

Traditions in youth work

To make sense of youth work we must explore the objects, ideas and practices that people make reference to when asked to explain what they think youth work is, and that are alluded to in the normal course of practice. We must examine use, for there are major problems in attempting lexical definition. Many of the elements that may be used to form any definition of youth work are problematic. Aims, the character of organization, processes utilized, client group, nature of the provider, and the form of relationship between user and provider could separately or collectively be used to form a definition. However, a review of current practice labelled and accepted as in some way being 'youth work', reveals an extraordinary range of differences and disputes (Jeffs and Smith, 1988a: 3–7). In a sense, it is more helpful to think of there being different and competing forms of youth work rather than a single youth work with commonly agreed characteristics. Yet youth work came to be recognized as having descriptive meaning and certain forms of practice were excluded from its embrace. This process of constructing and maintaining boundaries is central to an under-standing of youth work and the way in which the bargains which inform its operation came to be struck.

A number of bodies of customs, thoughts and practices appear to be important to practitioners when explaining and naming what they do. Initially, these may be thought of as traditions which have been handed down and worked upon. They help provide a model of reality or cognitive map for practitioners. For example, central to popular youth work are those traditions of practice which use social and leisure provision. These may begin from the commonsense position that young people have a need to meet, enjoy themselves and develop their leisure-time interests. However, many of these opportunities in the community are closed to young people because of age, expense or their 'safety'. There may also be a feeling that young people need space to be on their own, away from adults' eyes so that they can take on new roles, engage in new activities and enjoy themselves. In response to these perceived needs, practitioners try to provide places for young people to meet that are appropriately supervised and therefore seen as safe by other adults. They also provide opportunities for young people to develop their interests – to learn to enjoy themselves.

Social and leisure provision, as described here, presents us with a number of distinctive forms and symbols. There are particular conceptions of the worker's role, the direction of the work, what constitutes success, and the types of activity to be undertaken. These are among the constituents of tradition. However, there would appear to be at least two traditions: the first convivial and social and emphasizing atmosphere, and the second, rather more organized and self-consciously active (see Foreman, 1987; Eggleston, 1976).

The former tradition is expressed in a number of practice forms. A good example is the provision of an environment with a free and easy atmosphere a bit like a working men's club or pub. There is the coffee bar with comfortable seating, various machines and pub-type games, such as pool and darts, and music and dancing. As with pubs there may be some team games, especially football, although the emphasis on these will generally be on playing for enjoyment rather than winning. In many respects this tradition connects with what Foster (1977) described as the free-and-easy organizing style of mass working-class sub-culture in the mid-1800s (see Chapter 2).

One of the common ways of judging whether an evening or event has been successful is a recourse to the notion of 'atmosphere'. Workers make a judgement about the general ambience of the group – were people happy, were things 'happening', was there a 'buzz' and so on. This reference to atmosphere and sense of occasion and of things 'happening' is central. When workers talk of enjoyment, particular attitudes and behaviours are prized. First, there is usually a valuing of participation, of 'involvement'. Running alongside this is something of a celebration of community, the sense that young people are members of a group and of a wider society. Thirdly, there is usually an emphasis on friendship and relationships (particularly of the girl meets boy variety). Getting on well with one another also appears to be highly valued by workers. Underlying this is a general belief that people's opinions and needs should be respected, that things should be 'fair'. Finally, safety would seem to be an important consideration. The club, project or unit should seek to provide a non-exploitative and convivial environment in which young people can meet.

A key element in this tradition is the availability of 'sympathetic adults'. The sort of qualities that are valued in this conception are the ability to listen and not to prejudge, a respect for and a valuing of individuals and approachability. One of the common role models is that of friend or surrogate relative. This is perhaps borne of a limited access to different models of the relationship between adults and young people. Workers may 'know' that they are not teachers or social workers but are unable to find enough in the concept of 'youth worker' to explain their role.

The 'leisure'- as against the socially-orientated tradition provides activities in a more structured way. Here the concern may well be about developing people's interests or hobbies or extending their sporting abilities. The focus is not upon personal development in the broad sense, and the enjoyment that flows from the activity may come from the sense of doing something well, or at least better than before. Such an approach can take the form of specialist classes or sessions, or the formation of more focused clubs such as those for fishing, model railways, computing, photography, chess and a variety of sporting interests. Yet as soon as we begin to examine the operation of enthusiast clubs in any depth we find many of the values and practices used to characterize the social tradition. Such communal leisure groups provide (i) a means by which people with common enthusiasms can exchange information, guidance and specialist products, (ii) give opportunities for collective rather than individual projects (such as model railway layouts), and (iii) they

> provide opportunities for making friends and meeting people, suggesting that the substantive activity itself may be of secondary importance. . . . For many organizations this purely social dimension to their existence may not be quite legitimate to discuss openly but may shape their final identity far more than the nature and rules of their ostensible leisure activity. (Bishop and Hoggett, 1986: 33)

Further, within the various sub-cultures associated with the different activities, 'the phrase "pot-hunter" – someone whose sole imperative is to win trophies – appears to be used almost universally . . . as a form of abuse' (Bishop and Hoggett, 1986: 54). Competitive structures do not necessarily imply a dominance of competitive values. In contrast, it is loyalty, the 'good club wo/man' and the notion of the club as a valued social organization in its own right which is often important. It is these interconnections which allow us to consider these different traditions together.

Butters and Newell, when examining the 'cultural matrix' of the social education repertoire and its 'historical adjuncts' – character building and self-emancipation (the radical paradigm) – failed to recognize the importance and distinctiveness of social and leisure provision (1978: 38–46). However, this should not lead us to dismiss automatically the 'cultural matrixes' that they did identify. When these are examined in the context of practice it can be seen that within them are a number of competing and contrasting traditions. For example, it is possible to identify a number of traditions around character-building and these have frequently been manifested in different organizations and practices (Macleod, 1983). But although it is possible to list common elements such as physical exercise and discipline, restraints on sexuality, the encouragement of individual interests, and preparation for responsibility (Butters and Newell, 1978: 41; Roberts *et al.*, 1974), there are major and often bitter differences. Perhaps the best known of these is Baden Powell's criticism of the drill and militarism of the Boys' Brigade (Springhall *et al.*, 1983).

Within the character-building traditions are a number of strands of practice. A common approach, found in uniformed organizations, involves the provision of a clear hierarchical structure through which people move, and a range of activities and experiences to support the process. Achievement and movement through the organization are expressed in badges and their like. Careful thought is often given to the content of the training. Another strand contains the same emphasis on leadership, clarity of structure and purposeful activity, but does not utilize the trappings of uniform. Here the concern is to create an environment that is caring and in which 'people know where they are'. Leadership will often be 'by example'. It is more club-like and is perhaps most commonly seen in some elements of the Boys' Club movement (Dawes, 1975).

Yet another strand emphasizes collective performance and the building up of skills and attitudes which help that performance. It can be seen in some of the youth work that has a very strong sporting emphasis with a high value put on winning. It is interesting to note here the similarity in language and tone to that adopted by football managers: they often talk of 'character'; there was up until recently a concern to restrict their players' sexual activities before matches; hierarchy is all important (respect for the 'the boss'); and, of course, efforts must be harnessed for the good of the team ('it was a good all-round performance').

Similarly, the social education repertoire can be explored, although it may be more helpfully thought of as being concerned with personal and social development (see Chapter 5). In many respects the boundaries that Butters and Newell drew between cultural adjustment, community development and institutional reform can be seen to correspond with traditions of practice, although it is highly unlikely that those directly involved in them would name them such. One of the difficulties presumably encountered by Butters and Newell, was the distinction between these forms and those of social and leisure provision. Two immediate differences arise in use. First, there tends to be a focus on enjoyment in the social and leisure traditions, and upon development or improvement in the social and personal development traditions. The former tends to emphasize the present rather more than the latter. In other words, there is a concern that young people can enjoy themselves now, although to do that they have to learn certain rules and behaviours. Secondly, the appeal is made to everyday conceptions, as against professionalized conceptions, of role and theory. In the leisure tradition, as opposed to the social tradition, the developmental aspects will usually take a narrower front, based largely upon competence or involvement in a particular area of activity.

The search for a radical paradigm with its conceptualization of the youth work process as the 'sponsorship of peer-group support by helping sub-cultural groups enquire into their political history' (Butters and Newell, 1978: 39; see also Robins and Cohen, 1978) was the last matrix identified. While this may have been a tidy and logical step in the model, the totality does leave a range of politicized and collective practices outside its bounds. A number of traditions have had as their principal concern the development of people's political understanding, their ability to act politically and the creation of an identity with a particular view of the world and social movement. (M. Smith, 1987). These can be found in some of the activities of the early Co-operative Youth Movement, the Woodcraft Folk and in groups like the Clarion Scouts. In the 1920s and 1930s there was youth work development by political parties using organizations such as the Primrose League (Conservatives) and the Young Socialists. Recently, there have been major developments connected with the Women's and Black Consciousness Movements (Spence, 1988; Popple, 1988) and with political movements in particular communities, e.g. the Bangladeshi youth leagues (Carey and Shukur, 1986).

The nature of the work will very much depend on the way that politics is perceived. For example, those who see politics as being largely about government will tend to emphasize different questions from those who see politics as being about power relationships in society (M. Smith, 1987: 3–9). In recent times it is those with this broader view that have influenced many of the debates within youth work. Their desire could be seen as the provision of opportunities and structures in which people can come to understand their personal experiences of oppression as being both personal and political and can, as a consequence, take action both in the way they live their lives and in what has traditionally been seen as the political arena – the political parties, unions and so on. The narrower conception of politics may lead workers to seek to enable young people to campaign around a particular issue such as nuclear disarmament or to value specific political institutions such as the Party.

When the Butters and Newell framework is set alongside practice, two further ensembles of tradition appear to be missing. The first might be characterized as 'welfaring' and makes particular reference to thinking and practice within casework and counselling. Particular groups of young people are hence identified as being 'at risk', 'in trouble', 'deprived' or undergoing personal crisis. The welfaring solution is to provide specialist help to support those people with special needs through their difficulties and periods of crisis (Lawton, 1984; Masterson, 1982). This may take a number of forms, e.g. some agencies may tend to concentrate on a therapeutic approach, while other professional agencies may focus on 'helping'. Here there would appear to be three main concerns. The first is to help people to clarify, understand and act upon their problems. This work can happen in a variety of settings ranging from specialist 'advice' services, through various examples of project work, to clubs. A second aspect is the giving of advice, i.e. an actual opinion on the way that people should act. Thirdly, there is a straightforward giving of information, such as rights under the law, how to claim social security, etc. These last two approaches can be best seen in the work of advice and information centres. A further form that work in this tradition may take is the direct provision of material help in the form of money, meals or accommodation (Grafton, 1979).

Alongside the welfaring ensemble is that of rescue. In many respects it shares a parallel history, flowing in a direct line from the child-savers of the nineteenth century. The language, religious direction and the underlying view of young people and society is remarkably unchanged although, as might be expected, many of the practices have altered. The parallelling of 'welfaring' is hardly surprising given the roots of social work, but while casework gained massively from its courtship with the work of writers such as Freud, the rescuers remained within what could be called a proselytizing framework. Welfaring is primarily professionalized, whereas rescuing often assumes the mantle of a moral crusade. People are in need of saving and such judgements are based upon an ideology drawn from a particular social movement, often religious in nature. The problems faced are then seen not so much as structural, but as personal. The central deficit is often portrayed as emotional or moral (see Wilson, 1985).

Professions, people and movements

In what has been discussed so far we can discern six broad groupings of traditions and these are set out in Fig. 3.1. Broadly it can be said that welfaring and personal and social development are largely professional traditions. By this it is meant that they are mainly expounded and practised by occupational groups who

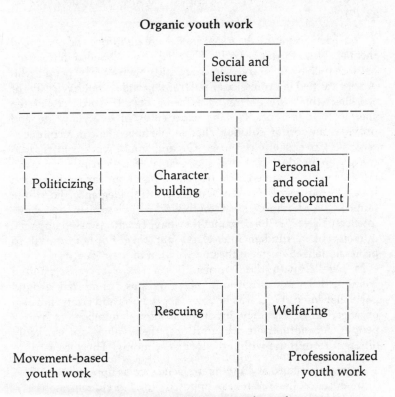

Fig. 3.1: *Traditions in youth work*

have attained a dominant position within their particular division of labour. Within advanced capitalist societies, Wilding has argued that the professions fulfil three functions. First, they stand as an expression of state concern for private troubles which have been accepted as public issues. Secondly, their expertise legitimates state action. Elites in capitalist societies have increasingly sought to rationalize and legitimate their control of all sorts of deviant and troublesome elements by consigning them to the attentions of experts. Thus expertise cloaks and legitimizes the exercise of state power. And, thirdly:

> the welfare professions provide a rich source of desirable jobs in the public and private sectors for members of elite and middle class groups where such groups can enjoy varying degrees of power, privilege and freedom in their work and, through their efforts, help to maintain the system which supports them in varying degrees of elegance. (Wilding, 1982: 17)

I have kept separate the social and leisure traditions and portrayed them as 'organic youth work'. They have been labelled in this way because such work is largely initiated and undertaken by people who are not steeped in professionalized training and do not have ways of working which are portrayed as being only the property of the specialist. It is rooted in the experiences of everyday life and provides the sort of 'solution' that people have made in a common-sense way over many centuries. Organic youth work is integral to the group producing it and its identity is primarily formed by reference to that immediate group. In terms of our earlier discussion it can be bourgeois or non-bourgeois in its allegiance. For those familiar with Gramsci, such youth workers are similar to 'organic intellectuals' (1971: 14–5) in that they have functions based upon the interests of a fundamental class, but they do not appeal to professionalized forms in the construction of their identity.

In parallel with these forms, lies a range of self-organized communal leisure provision. These groups, organized around particular interests such as hobbies, sports, arts and crafts, are also organic forms and they involve substantial numbers of young people. As mutual aid organizations, their values are markedly different from those within the formal economy. They are:

> values of reciprocity and interdependence as opposed to self-interest, collectivism as opposed to individualism, the importance of loyalty and a sense of 'identity' or 'belonging' as

opposed to the principle of forming ties on the basis of calculation, monetary or otherwise. (Bishop and Hoggett, 1986: 53)

While not wanting to romanticize the situation, much organic youth work can be similarly described and could be considered as an expression of mutual aid, depending upon the significance attached to the differences between the youth of its members and the adultness of its workers.

In recent years there has been a growing professional incursion into this area of social and leisure organization. This has applied to both self-conscious youth provision and to communal leisure organization. The development of municipal discos and dances, full-time youth social centres and sports and leisure centres may be seen as constituting a further tradition of practice, but largely holding markedly different values.

Finally, the character-building, rescuing and politicizing traditions are linked, although they have very different starting points and tend to serve vastly different visions of the status quo. They are bracketed together because all three traditions tend to have strong and explicit links with, and express their identities through, social movements of one kind or another. The term 'social movement' has a wide range of meanings attached to it and it is perhaps best to talk in terms of concrete examples. The political movements that have been of significance include the women's movement, the Black Consciousness movement, the labour and socialist movement and at times movements of the right such as the Fascists. Some youth organizations that could be to some extent located within this tradition have self-consciously taken on the title 'movement', e.g. the Gay Youth Movement (Trenchard and Warren, 1985; Kent-Baguley, 1988) and the Southall Youth Movement (CARF, 1981: 54). The scale of spontaneous, and later organized, developments within character and team building has led to their being movements in their own right, e.g., Scouting, Guiding and the Boys' Brigade.

In addition, it is crucial to recognize the major influence that religious groups have had upon the development of the different traditions of youth work. The connections between some of the non-conformist and evangelical churches and the development of the traditions of character-building and rescuing has already been noted. Within these traditions particular emphasis is placed upon encouraging young people's identity with the host or sponsoring movement. Where it comes to religion, that sense of identity is fundamental. Conversion is about changes or adaptations in form, character or function. Religious conversion means adopting particular attitudes, beliefs and behaviours; the movement or church is both a collective expression of belief and a means of sustaining that belief.

Religious groups will often sponsor work in the other ensembles of tradition. In doing so they may well be placing a value on the practical expression of belief or on catering for needs other than spiritual, rather than the desire for conversion or discipleship. Thus, a great deal of work within the social and leisure traditions is sponsored or subsidized by religious groups. Some of it will be directed at providing opportunities for enjoyment and social intercourse for the sons and daughters of the church, temple, mosque or group members, while some will be aimed at discharging a broader social responsibility that develops out of faith.

Three further points have to be made about the arrangement of the traditions in Fig. 3.1. First, there is a sense in which the professionalized traditions of welfaring, and social and personal development are mirrored by the movement traditions of rescue, and character and team building. The 'pairs' do share some common characteristics, but their placement in professional or movement traditions are the result of very real differences: differences which are often related to the desire within movement-based approaches for young people to make an explicit ideological commitment to the movement itself.

Secondly, the politicizing traditions have been placed on one side because of the contested and marginal position that they have occupied within youth work practice. There has been considerable debate as to whether they can be considered as youth work (M. Smith, 1987: 26–7).

Thirdly, the vast bulk of what we know as youth work would fall into one of the triangle of traditions at the top of the diagram – character building, social and leisure provision, and social and personal development. The central or dominant traditions of non-uniformed youth work are those of social and leisure provision. Within uniformed organizations, such as Scouting, it is possible to find work which appeals both to the notion of 'character-building' and yet uses many of the ideas and methods associated with social and leisure provision and personal and social development. One view of this overlapping might be that youth work has entered a particular historical period, where the dominant model of practice is that of personal and social development or social and leisure provision, and that other models such as that of character-building have been pushed to the sidelines. This might be one reading of Butters and Newell (1978). But such a view does not seem tenable as the range of thinking and practice within youth work is extremely wide. As Taylor (1987) has argued, the character-building traditions are not the spent force that some would have us believe. Within Scouting there has been a significant call to 'get back to 'basics' (Walsh, 1982) and elements of Intermediate Treatment practice, with their emphasis on challenge and character, are very close to these traditions. Such 'overlapping' can be better understood as the powerful reinterpretation of particular character-building traditions. The orientation may have changed, but the symbols forms of expression and organizational structures remain essentially the same.

Traditions, boundaries and change

Traditions give workers a place in the world. Practitioners will share ideas and practices and these in turn will be distinguishable in some significant way from those of other groupings. In this way they may be seen as 'establishing or symbolizing social cohesion or the membership of groups, real or artificial communities' (Hobsbawm, 1984: 9). Other, overlapping types of tradition establish or legitimize institutions, status or relations of authority, or have socialization as their main purpose, i.e. 'the inculcation of beliefs, value systems and conventions of behaviour' (Hobsbawm, 1984).

Both similarity and differences are implied in these traditions. Hence, they express a relational idea, the opposition of one tradition to others or to other social constructions. This places considerable importance upon boundaries – the marking of the beginning and the end of the tradition. These boundaries do indeed constitute critical breaks. The way in which they are marked will depend upon the nature of the tradition. As Cohen has noted, the symbols employed to mark the boundary do more than merely stand for or represent something else:

> Indeed if that was all they did, they would be redundant. They also allow those who employ them to supply part of their meaning. . . . Age, life, father, purity, gender, death, doctor are all symbols shared by those who share the same language, or participate in the same symbolic behaviour through which these categories are expressed and marked. But their meanings are *not* shared in the same way. Each is mediated by the idio-syncratic experience of the individual. (Cohen, 1985: 14; emphasis as in original)

Thus, the boundaries between traditions may be understood as being constructed in the minds of their beholders and, as such, may be experienced in very different ways, not only by those on opposing sides of the boundary, but also by those on the same side. The capacity for symbols such as club, character, leader and Christ to have varying meanings attached to them is one source of their strength. Styles of dress, ways of greeting, forms of activity and types of building can be viewed similarly. Their very imprecision as symbols makes for effectiveness as they permit interpretation and provide scope for manoeuvre by those who use them:

> Symbols . . . 'express' other things in a way which allow their common form to be retained and shared among the members of a group, whilst not imposing upon these people the constraints of a uniform meaning. Because symbols are malleable in this way, they can be made to 'fit' the circumstances of the individual. (Cohen, 1985: 18)

Yet while meanings may be relatively unspecified, the practices which are symbolized are often compulsory, such as the flag ritual in American schools: 'The crucial element seems to have been the invention of emotionally and symbolically charged signs of club membership rather than the statutes and objects of the club' (Hobsbawm, 1984: 11).

Great care has to be taken when approaching apparently long-standing forms, for while the outward symbol may remain unchanged and accepted, the meanings attached to it alter and can conflict. In this way the notion of 'traditions' helps us to understand why there is so much in youth work that does not appear to have changed significantly, and why practitioners with apparently different perspectives and practices identify with each other. While the form has remained reasonably constant, or at least recognizable, the content can vary. Immediately this is apparent when examining the traditions associated with Scouting. The idea of the 'camp' is particularly strong – the form is familiar over time, as are many of the routines and practices, yet the way in which notions associated with it are understood, such as leadership and challenge, have changed. Here again the notion of boundary is important, for while within particular traditions the complexity of meanings attached to different symbols may to some extent be appreciated, when viewed from the outside the form can beguile the onlooker. Externally a particular youth work tradition will often be explained in terms of a number of simple stereotypes.

At times of change, when 'everything that may have been stable is caught up into transformation and development; [and] all that is solid . . . melts into air' (Wright, 1985: 16), traditions are an anchor. Indeed, when groupings such as those involved in youth work turn to 'history' or stress tradition, this is often indicative of dislocation and anxieties about change. In this respect, it should not be forgotten that many traditions are not simply handed down but are actually invented. In Scouting we have a clear example of this process as Baden Powell strove to establish traditions of ritual and ceremony.

Traditions provide stability and legitimacy. However, they are also invoked to justify change. Thus, in many of the papers and reports that have argued for the development of work with young women and girls, for example, great play has been made of the long-established 'tradition' of single-sex work and its achievements, even though much of the invoked 'tradition' was directed at the domestication of young women. In other words, the past is selectively invoked and constructed in order to articulate contemporary concerns. The use of traditions in this way, in part, accounts for their relative permanence: they are kept alive and refreshed by the innovations practitioners make. At club or unit level, traditions can become established over quite a short period of time. They may take the form of stories that are recounted in order to explain why things are done or should be done in a particular way. Alternatively, tradition may be manifested in the procedures that have to be followed, i.e. 'this is the way things are done here'.

In each tradition there is an appeal to different sources for the legitimation of practice and a resort to different forms of theory and models concerning the worker's role. Traditions offer a broad range of ideas, institutions and customs. Practitioners therefore have to look elsewhere for further 'explanations' of the things they should do. Youth work's marginal position, lying as it does on the boundaries of a number of activities, means that it is possible for workers to draw upon a significant range of theories from other areas about the practitioner's role and purpose. This is not helped by the lack of theory making within youth work itself. What is apparent, is that within and across traditions, workers appeal to different bodies of theory to explain their practice. They use examples and dispositions which transcend youth work. This, added to the malleability of symbols, allows workers with seemingly conflicting orientations to be located in the same tradition.

Some people operating within the character-building traditions may see themselves as educators, some of those within the politicizing traditions as proselytizers, and so on. For this reason it is sometimes difficult to distinguish between different examples of practice. In the end it is likely that individuals will find their identity as practitioners through a particular tradition and the utilization of specific symbols. In this way the traditions are important, but so are the transcending influences which contribute to the range of meanings attached to any one symbol within a tradition. By pointing to the nature of the contact that workers have with the people they work with, the symbols and values they might draw upon when intervening and what are the conditions prevalent, we can begin to see how traditions may interact with other aspects of the youth work process, and how everyday necessities can dispose workers to particular systems of thought.

In conclusion

In this chapter I have tried to develop a system for the naming of the different strands of youth work practice and thinking which reflect the experiences of workers. These ways of seeing and acting in the world of youth work – characterized as traditions – will be recognizable to those that manage and sponsor the work and those that make use of it. However, as recognizable as these traditions may be, they will not necessarily name the way that young people or sponsors see things. What they do help explain is the apparent continuity of youth work and the way in which workers may, at times, make an appeal to the same bodies of theory and practice and yet set themselves apart. They also show how people with apparently very different practices and understandings see themselves as connected.

What this tentative categorization also achieves, is the proper recognition of the social and leisure traditions and their central place in youth work practice and thinking. These traditions have tended to become buried in some representations, and stereotyped and dismissed in others. They are the dominant traditions in youth work and deserve careful consideration, for they possess a number of features which make them an important focus when considering the shape of future practice.

Chapter 4

The Demise of
the Youth Service?

There cannot have been a time in the history of youth work when someone did not speak of crisis. Such concerns have involved the 'problems' that young people presented, the impact of economic, political or social change upon society in general or young people in particular, or difficulties about the funding, organization and recognition of the work. The idea of crisis is perhaps best exemplified by the case of someone who is ill; it is 'a turning point in the course of the illness, but also a period of heightened danger and uncertainty. The person may recover, or may die' (Hill and Bramley, 1986: 78). While the notion of crisis may be overworked, such is the uncertainty both in the environment in which youth workers operate and in the work itself, that the demise of the Youth Service – and along with it certain elements of youth work – now appears a strong possibility. The point has been reached where a relatively smooth continuance looks impossible: the position of young people has worsened; welfare in general has come under attack and there have been major shifts in welfare policy; and there are deep problems concerning purpose and theory within the Service.

Growing inequality and a new social condition of youth?

There is little need to describe at length the scale and nature of the economic restructuring which is currently taking place in the UK. The declining manufacturing base, the relative shift of employment into service industries, the internationalization of production and distribution, the utilization of ever more capital-intensive methods

of production, and the movement away from the established manufacturing centres have not only contributed to the desolation of
whole regions but have also heightened social differences in general.
In the first half of the 1980s, unemployment more than doubled and
pay differentials widened considerably. At the same time changes in
taxation and in the dispersement and overall levels of social security
benefits contributed to a real cut in income for the poorest sections of
the community (Mack and Lansley, 1985; Rentoul, 1987). This
situation has been further aggravated by another shift in housing
policy towards the relative subsidy of those buying their own
homes:

> The problem is not only huge, however, it is also desperately
> serious for many. Among the 7.5 million people living in
> poverty, there are some 2.5 million people, including nearly 1
> million children, whose lives are diminished and demeaned in
> *every* way so far as they fall below the minimum standards of
> society today. (Mack and Lansley, 1985: 282–3)

In addition to these general shifts, the employment situation
facing young people has been worsened by technical advances which
have destroyed some traditional teenage jobs, by the allegedly high
cost to employers of the wages paid to young workers, and by
official policy, which has invested money in 'training' rather than
job creation (Coffield *et al.*, 1986: 206–7). The scale of the problem
has been further exacerbated by Government action, as Allbeson has
noted in respect of income maintenance: during the first half of the
1980s a low priority was attached to protecting the incomes of young
people; there was an added delay in the recognition of adult
independence for the unemployed by the state; and the transfer of
support for those on benefit from the state to the family, with little
acknowledgement of the financial burden which resulted (Allbeson,
1985: 81–2). This situation has continued (Jeffs and Smith, 1988a:
51–2).

Whatever the reasons for this apparent lack of priority for youth,
it has been argued that the result is a devastation of work prospects,
and hence wages, for a large group of young people, which is also a
devastation of their future: 'The wage . . . is the means to, and
promise of a future. It is the crucial pivot for social and cultural
transitions into what this society defines as adulthood' (Willis *et al.*,
1985: 218). In this way the young unemployed have been pushed
into a 'new social condition' of suspended animation between school
and work with an extended period of relative poverty and
dependency upon the family and on the state. This process,

according to Coffield *et al.*, has the effect of intensifying the 'customary roles of young women as domestic labourers' (1986: 205). It has confirmed the disadvantage suffered by black young people who experience disproportionate unemployment rates compared with white people, and considerable discrimination in the operation of training schemes (Newnham, 1986: 17–20). The social consequences of all this are still to be calculated: 'the almost endless adolescence, which for decades has become the lot of middle class youth, is now the daily experience of their working class contemporaries with one critical distinction: for the latter there will be no elite jobs to compensate for the long denial of status' (Coffield *et al.*, 1986: 205).

The idea that this is a *new* social condition needs approaching with care, as it can easily become used as a metaphor for a generation. What is claimed as new looks depressingly old and is brought about by the intensification of existing conditions in times of mass unemployment. After all, racial discrimination hardly began with the onset of mass unemployment. Further, the scale and extent of the condition needs putting in context. Most people in their early 20s are employed, live in reasonable, or at least adequate housing, and enjoy a standard of living which surpasses that which pertained two decades earlier. This is not to deny that large numbers of young people have been disadvantaged significantly over the last decade. Nor is it to minimize the changes that have occurred since the 1950s in terms of young people's employment, training and education. However, it is only by considering these dimensions, that we can begin to see why increased social disadvantage has not caused undue alarm to successive Conservative governments. From their perspective, the handling of youth unemployment, for example, has been an area of considerable success. The objects of excluding a greater proportion of young people from the labour market and lowering their income levels and expectations, without incurring a major threat to order or undermining the Government's political base, have been achieved (Jeffs and Smith, 1988a: 47–56).

Welfare crisis?

Any government faces considerable problems in a recession for, as O'Higgins (1985) has argued, the absence of growth eliminates the augmentation of resources from which increased social expenditure (and thus it was assumed, increased redistribution) could be financed, without cutting into pre-tax living standards. Without growth, redistribution requires real losses for some (O'Higgins,

1985: 163). Recession also increases the demands upon the social welfare system and reduces the numbers of people who pay tax and make social insurance contributions. While the costs involved in having over three million unemployed are huge, with demographic changes the government also faces a growing bill for pensions and social services for the elderly (Tinker, 1981: 12–3).

Some, such as O'Connor (1973), have argued that Western capitalist states are experiencing a fiscal crisis, and that there is a continual conflict between classes over the goals and forms of social policy and a 'contradictory process through time as the growth of the welfare state contributes to new forms of crisis' (Gough, 1979: 15). Furthermore, the range and depth of criticism directed at the performance and direction of welfare policy would appear to indicate that the broad consensus concerning the mixed economy and the Welfare State, which has apparently characterized many Western societies since the Second World War, has cracked. Writers such as Mishra (1984) have suggested that the Welfare State is faced with a crisis of legitimacy. Keynesian-Beveridge style social theories are judged to have lost credibility. From the right, it has been argued that welfare policies are a massive burden on the economy, that they attract scarce resources away from more productive uses (Bacon and Eltis, 1976) and that welfare programmes are inefficient and indiscriminating in coverage (Harris and Seldon, 1979). The growth of the women's movement, the continuing development of black political organizations, and the various examples of action regarding disability and sexuality have also contributed to the critique of welfare. Social policy can, thus be examined as 'a set of structures created by men to shape the lives of women' (Wilson, 1983: 33). Well-intentioned multicultural initiatives can be seen as 'functioning as a means of diffusing difficult inner-city school situations and as an attempt to pacify black communities' (Sarup, 1986: 111). Finally, the extent to which the State has been able, and has the potential, to achieve significant redistribution to those in need is a theme taken up by a number of writers committed to a more equitable distribution, such as Townsend and Davidson (1982). Indeed, Le Grand (1982) suggests that the rich benefit disproportionately from free or subsidized public services. Thus, public expenditure on health care, education, housing and transport is shown to favour systematically the better off and to maintain inequality (Le Grand, 1982: 137).

To what extent all this constitutes a 'crisis' in welfare is open to debate. There is a major empirical question mark against the idea of a fiscal crisis (Hill and Bramley, 1986: 87) and it may be, as Taylor-Gooby (1985) has argued, that it is the continuities rather than the cleavages and conflicts that provide the dominant theme. In his view, it is factors outside the Welfare State which are significant, such as the pursuit of a monetarist economic policy (which produces higher levels of unemployment), rather than changes in the constitution and organization of welfare (Taylor-Gooby, 1985: 91). However, the general attack upon welfare, combined with demographic changes and the impact of the recession has had a particular effect upon youth work. First, there are simply fewer young people around. A club with a nightly average attendance of fifty 14–16 year olds in 1971, could expect 37 in 1988. Secondly, as we have seen, particular groups of young people have been affected disproportionately by the economic and social impact of recession. Thirdly, the general attack on welfare spending involved a per capita cut in expenditure upon the Youth Service in the region of 8–10 per cent in the first half of the 1980s (D.I. Smith, 1985). In the wake of the 1987 election and with a concern to 'tackle' the inner-cities, Grant-related Expenditure Assessments for youth work were increased substantially and showed a 38 per cent increase to 1990. However, on the previous occasion such an increase was indicated, following the 1981 riots, it did not materialize. Where additional monies have become available they are often tied to specific initiatives. Fourthly, although privatization and other New Right schemes have not, as yet, substantially infiltrated Youth Service provision, they have affected the context in which youth workers operate. The massive expansion of commercial leisure provision and the targeting of resources away from general youth work into more specialized arenas are aspects of this. None the less, the major voluntary presence within youth work has meant that it could be portrayed as an example of the very welfare pluralism which many on the right wish to promote, and this has perhaps shielded it from some criticism (Jeffs and Smith, 1988a: 42–3). However, there are, as Shaw *et al.* (1988) have suggested, a range of possible targets for further privatization attempts. Finally elements of the welfare critique have entered the discourse of youth work and have found some expression in the development of work with girls and young women (Carpenter and Young, 1986) and with young black people (John, 1981). All this can be seen in the way youth work has become organized.

Youth work organization and the development of parallel provision

Within much of the discussion about youth work, the Albemarle

Report (HMSO, 1960) has attained special significance. It is seen as a
watershed, whose importance went beyond the boost it gave to the
resources available to the work. Davies, for example, presents it as
seeking to adapt youth work's image, style and philosophy to a new
age and especially to a new youth culture (1986: 99). The Report is
sometimes advanced as heralding a golden age of youth work, where
workers and trainers were confident in their actions, where
resources flowed into buildings and staffing, and where there was
some intellectual debate about theory and practice. However, as
Jeffs has argued, the influence of the Albemarle Report was probably
far more symbolic than real, providing the government with a public
raison d'être for policies that were largely pre-ordained (1979: 46)
and an approach to basic structural problems that was suitably
depoliticized. The Youth Service was seen as having two central
functions: (i) the socialization and social education of the mass of
young people. Much of this became couched in the language of
smoothing the transition from school to work; and (ii) the control
and containment of a deviant minority (Jeffs and Smith, 1987b). As
with much that had gone before, the problems addressed were
essentially perceived as concerning working-class young people,
although given the prevalent intellectual climate, they were not
presented in this way. The chipping away by other agencies at the
contribution made by the Youth Service to these two functions has
contributed to the non-emergence of a distinctive youth work
profession and the impasse that the Service now finds itself in (Jeffs
and Smith, 1987b, 1988a). In order to understand the threat now
posed to the Youth Service it is necessary to address these
arguments.

In 1959 the majority of young people in the designated age range
of the Youth Service were in employment. With the raising of the
school-leaving age to 16 and increased levels of voluntary staying-on
or transference to further education and training, a growing
proportion of the client group are now in full-time education. Much
of what youth workers described as 'social education' became
available through the normal school curriculum (see Chapter 5).
Further, the re-emergence of mass youth unemployment has led to
the creation of a range of programmes designed to ease the transition
from school to either employment or unemployment (Finn, 1987).
The combination of these with the expansion of higher education
means that the large majority of those who had previously been seen
as the clients of the Youth Service are no longer within the traditional
labour market. Thus, agencies now exist that have the ability to
deliver the priorities expressed by Albemarle in a more direct way.

Alongside this expansion in formal provision, there has been a substantial increase in the amount of school-based youth work. The advocacy of such provision by the Fairbairn-Milson Report (DES, 1969), the cost advantages which accompany it, and the growing persuasiveness to policy makers of the rhetoric and practice of community education, undoubtedly helped fuel this expansion. Indeed, the Fairbairn Sub-committee (as opposed to the Milson Sub-committee), concluded that 'the concept of youth service as a separate system should be allowed to atrophy' (Fairbairn Report, 1968: para 301, quoted in Davies, 1986). While the resulting report struck a note of compromise, Fairbairn's conclusion looks close to the real situation in the late 1980s, although not necessarily for all the reasons advanced then. In Scotland the Youth Service has been incorporated into Community Education. In England, by 1980, perhaps 30–40 per cent of statutory youth provision was school-based (Booton, 1980: 78). Certainly there has been a major increase in the regular usage of schools for youth work (Jeffs and Smith, 1988a: 123).

The second element of Albemarle's vision for the Youth Service, the containment and control of troublesome youth, has increasingly become the property of more specialist agencies. The Youth Service did not deliver what was promised for it, and governments could not be seen to allow the panics about youth to be tackled by an agency that had neither legal powers to intervene nor a history of effective intervention (Jeffs and Smith, 1987b). One aspect of this has been the development of more specialized agencies such as those concerned with Intermediate Treatment (IT) (Adams, 1988). Although IT was initially envisaged as being closely linked to existing youth provision, the involvement of the Youth Service never materialized on any scale. New agencies, notably the local authority personal social service departments, augmented by organizations directly funded by central government, came to play a central role.

When we place the two elements together, three trends are immediately apparent. First, young people are increasingly being accommodated in services with a substantial legal framework, and are increasingly being compelled to undertake such activities. The raising of the school-leaving age, the expansion of further and higher education, participation on YTS, intermediate treatment and attendance orders are examples of this trend. In comparison, the delivery of Youth Service provision looks distinctly hit or miss. Secondly, there has been a growing differentiation and specialization of services and provision. A number of agencies and activities have emerged which claim some unique or defined purpose and clientele. In part, this is connected with the third broad trend, the relative development of professional groupings within parallel areas when compared with youth work. While undoubtedly social workers, teachers and probation officers experience many uncertainties and complexities in their work, there is a sense in which they each possess distinctive occupational cultures and a sense of their own importance and purpose. They have benefited from an extension of training and continuing developments in their literature and theory. This is not something that can be claimed for youth work. However, the question of prefessionalization cannot be left there, for there has been a substantial anti-professionalism expressed by key elements of the New Right and the Left. Within youth work, both views have combined to help stifle the growth of a distinctive youth work profession (Davies, 1988; Jeffs and Smith, 1987b). This would not matter if there had been a corresponding emphasis on developing and sustaining the craft of youth work, but unfortunately other factors have conspired against this.

Other agencies have entered the Youth Service's traditional preserve of leisure provision on a substantial scale. The growth of play provision, often funded through 'borough' as against 'county' authorities, and sited within a leisure, rather than educationally orientated department is a significant example in this respect. Indeed, it is the expansion of municipal leisure provision, whether in the form of sports and recreation centres, neighbourhood centres, youth-orientated events or through straightforward colonization, that is one of the distinctive features of the period. By the early 1980s, local authorities were spending over £600 million per year on recreational services (Hendry, 1983: 114). This shift of expenditure was apparently reflected in young people's leisure usage, with one survey showing that while 29 per cent of the young people interviewed regularly went to a youth club, some 47 per cent regularly went to sports centres (DES, 1983b: 74). Paradoxically, the development of school-based youth work has also strengthened this emphasis upon leisure. A large number of school-based initiatives are primarily concerned with encouraging participation and some competence in organized leisure activities, often of a sporting or craft nature (DES, 1986: 5, 1983a: 13; Welsh Office, 1986).

Commercial provision has also expanded spectacularly. While some mass leisure forms such as the cinema and dance-hall have declined, many others have arrived in their place. Television, music, tobacco, alcohol, gambling, tourism and even sex are packaged and presented as commodities to be bought and are often sold as a means of enhancing one's individuality (Rojek, 1985: 20). Thus, if we take just one area of commercial provision targetted at young people, the 'theme pub', we can see how they have been designed to appeal to different age ranges within the youth market, and to express different tastes. However, a common feature within this growing differentiation of provision is the attempt to provide young people with the artefacts of 'adulthood' (such as alcohol), alongside the provision of environments in which they can associate with their peers, free from persistent intrusion.

The growing differentiation and expansion of leisure provision, both commercial and public, has not only presented problems for the generic youth club, but for the Youth Service in general. The political and professional consciousness around leisure has had important ramifications in the way in which youth work is perceived. For example, a number of policy responses to youth unemployment appear to have worked on the assumption that recreation can be a direct substitute for work and have expected the Youth Service to act accordingly. This places it in a difficult position not only because it is exactly this age group that youth workers have difficulties in attracting to their provision but, rather more fundamentally, because work performs functions that leisure, as it is currently understood, is inherently incapable of fulfilling (Roberts, 1983: 188). Leisure provision cannot structure time and confer status and identity in the way that jobs do. Further, as Roberts (1983) comments, offering the young unemployed leisure skills and facilities is clearly a second-best palliative.

More generally, there are at least two distinctive movements concerning the relation of youth work organization and leisure provision. On the one hand, there is the introduction of informal work with young people at sports and leisure centres, perhaps as a response to problems posed by young people in such provision. On the other hand, existing youth provision has itself increasingly adopted a distinctive leisure ideology and hence facilitated provision on a commercial or 'activity' basis. Many existing youth centres are actually little more than public halls, effectively hiring out rooms to particular activity groups and providing informal educational provision for an increasingly small number of people. Redesignating such premises as community or youth halls, replacing full-time youth workers with part-time caretakers and administrators and turning premises for use over to autonomous groups or profit or non-profit making organizations can make a lot of sense to cost-conscious councils. In fact, such action may well increase the overall usage by young people, but in doing so effectively excludes others. Perhaps in recognition of such factors, a number of authorities have relocated their youth work under leisure services. Birmingham, Liverpool and Avon being examples of this in recent years.

These developments in youth policy would appear to have led towards vocationalism (and, as a consequence, leisurism), treatment, and policing and punishment. Cohen has argued that the emphasis given to 'skilling' in both the secondary school curriculum and 16–19 training provision, is primarily about the inculcation of social discipline. It represents 'an attempt to construct a more mobile form of self-discipline, adapted to changing technologies of production and consumption, and to link this to a modern version of self-improvement aimed at the reserve army of youth labour' (1984: 104). The same stress on 'skilling' can be found within many of the developments associated with leisurism and it would be a mistake to view the growth in leisure provision as simply providing displacement opportunities for those out of work. Such provision also makes a contribution to social discipline, both as a reward to those who have adopted appropriate values and behaviours and as an inducement to those who have not.

Alongside the emphasis upon vocationalism and leisure, there has been a continuing expansion in what might be termed treatment activities of which IT is a prime example, and a shift away from the welfaring approaches of the 1960s (Rutherford, 1986: 54–66). However, the movement has not stopped there and policing and punishment solutions have gathered momentum. This latter shift is not only concerned with an increased police role in 'preventative' activities, but also with, for example, the redefinition of the 'drug problem' as requiring a policing rather than medical solution (Davies, 1986: 121).

Crucially, in all this, the central State has adopted an increasingly interventionist role. At a local level, the movement towards more centralized control has been expressed in the workings of the corporate structures of local government with departmental committees and officers losing a degree of discretion. However, it is not simply a matter of corporatism, the most significant developments in terms of youth policy have been the massive growth of the Manpower Services Commission and, more recently, the debates about the core curriculum. The MSC has been important because it:

> increasingly defined for all other youth agencies such key problems and concerns as youth unemployment, skill shortages and indeed skill itself. By the mid 1980s, the MSC was . . . breaching some of the most resistant of organizational boundaries. Indeed its activities were threatening to

undermine the very institution of schooling as handed down from the 19th century and to eliminate the contradictory purposes and relatively relaxed forms of accountability built into these key state instruments for socializing the young. (Davies, 1986: 117)

Whether this is a reflection of a coherent and central youth policy or that governments now have the means to impose a range of centrally determined policies is a matter of argument. Part of the problem is that we have a great deal of circumstantial material concerning trends in different areas of welfare that are directed at young people, but little direct evidence of there being a concrete and coherent policy. There are certain commonalities and distinct trends, the relative power balance between agencies appears to have altered and certainly the impact of MSC thinking and programmes has been profound. However, we must also note the considerable resistance by elements of certain state agencies, such as the DES, to the introduction of some of the measures (Salter and Tapper, 1981). In addition, there have been a number of parallel trends which may contribute towards an apparently growing convergence of welfare practice, but may not, in themselves, be the direct result of government policy. One example of this is the movement towards 'nationalized' notions of 'good practice' associated with the growing professionalization of the areas under discussion (Shaw *et al.*, 1988). Further, we must ask to what extent are changes in programme and direction more crucially related to the deeper workings of the economy? Are in fact state policies and programmes better understood as arising, in a significant part, from knee-jerk reactions to what is occurring in the economic sphere? The trends would appear to suggest that a broad government policy towards young people does exist, but the extent to which this is coherent and is able to be centrally directed remains questionable.

Problems of purpose, theory and practice

The future would look less problematic if the Youth Service itself did not possess severe 'internal' difficulties. In this respect, HMI Reports on youth work provision make depressing reading. Ritchie concludes, after reviewing a number of these, that:

Given the lack of policies, aims and objectives, and criteria for evaluation that the Inspectors have identified, it comes as no particular surprise that youth club programmes everywhere are characterized by "ad hoc recreational activity". They are

. . . usually dominated by sport and physical recreation. This is a particular concern since these activities are often just played for themselves and not for any underlying, or even remotely visible, educational objectives. The Inspectors seem to be unhappy with most of what goes on in youth clubs and centres, finding the activities traditional and unchallenging – with one or two well-documented and admired exceptions. (Ritchie, 1986: 2–3)

Perhaps one of the best indicators of the malaise in practice is the consistent failure of the bulk of provision to address the requirements of young women and girls (Nava, 1984; N. Smith, 1984). Research conducted by ILEA (1984) in the first half of the 1980s showed that the position had not changed much since the last significant piece of research undertaken some 20 years earlier (Hanmer, 1964), even though there had supposedly been a growth in awareness concerning young women's needs and the ways in which youth workers might intervene. The researchers concluded that 'there is considerable sex stereotyping of activities – both in provision and in the extent to which one sex predominates in participation' (ILEA, 1984: 11). They found that many girls were not happy about the activities provided at their clubs and centres. Girls 'complained that most of the activities were dominated by boys and that boys would not allow them to participate. They also complained that the activities were orientated towards the interests of boys rather than girls' (ILEA, 1984: 16). On the whole there does not appear to have been substantial dialogue with young people concerning the provision of which they are a part.

Hanmer had earlier commented that the 'difficulty of catering for girls' in clubs was not a problem of knowledge, but one of attitudes, values and expectations (1964: 17). She suggested that the tendency of workers to think in mutually exclusive categories such as passive/active, clubbable/unclubbable implied a system of values which gave approval to boys and non-approval to girls, and this stood in the way of girls being catered for in clubs. This process of putting things into one of two 'boxes', of tending to think in an 'either/or' way, limits the ability to act and is somewhat reminiscent of something that Goodman once wrote about America:

In our society, bright lively children, with the potentiality for knowledge, noble ideals, honest effort, and some kind of worthwhile achievement, are transformed into useless and cynical bipeds, or decent young men trapped or early resigned, whether in or out of the organized system . . . it is desperately hard these days for an average child to grow up to be a man, for our present organized system of things does not want men. They are not safe. They do not suit. (Goodman, 1960: 23)

Perhaps it is that the expressed needs of young people do not fit youth workers' 'organized system of things'? By this I mean that many practitioners' whole way of thinking may well be at fault. (Much as Goodman's was when he talks of 'men' rather than 'adults'.) Thus, while young women have consistently stated what they require of youth work, their voice has remained essentially unheard. What they have been saying has not fitted the way most workers, trainers and policy makers see the world.

Thinking about purpose

Those unfamiliar with the Youth Service will often comment upon the apparently confusing array of purposes which organizations profess to serve. It is a feeling not confined to the passing observer, while, for example, the Review Group on the Youth Service in England was able to report that the submissions displayed 'a remarkable unanimity about the aims and philosophy of the Service' (HMSO, 1982: 27), as soon as the surface is disturbed, highly con-tested and under-conceptualized features appear:

Virtually all the respondents saw the Youth Service as an educational one. While the term social education was not usually defined, the aim of the process was clearly seen as helping the young person on the path to maturity, with partici-pation in leisure-time activity as the main agent. (HMSO, 1982: 27)

Unanimity can only be sustained when statements such as this are kept at a high level of generality and when they are recognized by participants as rhetoric. This is amply displayed by the Review Group Report which, no more than a couple of paragraphs after declaring unanimity about aims and philosophy, finds that submissions 'frequently stated . . . a lack of cohesion and sense of direction in the Service prevented the resources that were available from being used to the greatest advantage' (HMSO, 1982). This is a situation echoed by many local policy reviews (D.I. Smith, 1987), which is hardly surprising, given that within each of the main youth work traditions there will be a disposition to rather different views of youth work's essential purpose (see Chapter 3), and given the contradictory nature of many State activities (Jeffs and Smith,

1988a: 14–40). Here we will focus on the impact of this upon the front-line.

In much of the discussion about purpose, key words appear such as 'leadership', 'adulthood' and 'maturity'. Such words are important not so much as guides to action, but as symbols which provide some identity to the tradition in which the work is located (see Chapter 3). It is only by thoroughly interrogating the tradition that some direct and operational sense of purpose may appear. This can be highly problematical for workers. What should be a key reference point in their practice gives little direct guidance and for them to go further can entail considerable effort. This is an effort made doubly difficult by the lack of appropriate theory to which notions of purpose would have to connect. The fact that there is not an adequate theory or definition of social education, for example, does rather devalue any statement of purpose which includes the notion (see Chapter 5).

Moreover, of course, the simple fact that youth work organization is 'there' and 'doing something' (combined with a worker's immersion in the daily routine of activities, programming and administration) tends not to encourage reflection about purpose. When that daily routine is disturbed, when there is some form of crisis created by, for example, falling membership or 'trouble' in the sessions, then debate about direction may follow. A further factor here is the part-time and voluntary nature of the vast bulk of the labour force. Groups of workers may be operating in relative isolation, relying on commonsense understandings and with little time for what they might perceive as the luxury of thinking about aims.

In addition, full- and part-time workers generally do not have clear strategies for managing the practice and policy of their organizations, as do few local authorities. In reports this has often been expressed as a lack of management skills (see HMSO, 1982: 87–93). While there may indeed be a skill problem, there is also the question of identity and orientation, i.e. the extent to which workers perceive themselves as managers – whether of self, others, or an organization. Those individual face-to-face workers who understand they have a responsibility to manage their own interventions with young people will be more likely to ask questions about purpose.

Furthermore, and whatever the rhetoric may proclaim, there has been a general, although not universal, drift towards the idea that youth work exists to provide safe opportunities for young people to enjoy themselves. The movement towards recreation, with its hedonistic connotations, is rarely free from some lingering desire for the encouragement of improvement. It is also hedged around by other concerns, e.g. sexual behaviour, gambling, the use of drugs and stimulants such as alcohol, tobacco and other illegal substances, and a general protection from some forms of exploitation. Youth workers have never been able to pursue enjoyment with quite the single-mindedness that commercial operators might. As Roberts has commented, 'the staple role of leisure provision is offering environments where young people "can do their own things". The commercial sector has never found leadership a profitable formula' (1983: 178).

The vacuum that all this creates does leave Youth Service organizations highly susceptible to demands that some response should be made to whatever the current moral panic concerning young people may be (Marsland, 1978: 143). If youth work agencies are unclear about what their primary task is, then it becomes extremely difficult to judge whether a prospective piece of work is worth doing. Things are rushed into because they seem like a good idea – a common rationalization being 'we are trying to meet people's needs'. Given that any action is capable of being justified as meeting someone's needs somewhere, this is a more than suspect approach. Indeed, it is often the desire for organizational survival, rather than any perceived purpose in connection with young people, that is the major motivation for action. There is often money available for those who can be seen to be contributing to a quick 'solution' of a moral panic, but therein lies the catch. When, for example, the Albemarle Report (HMSO, 1960) offered youth work as a 'solution' for adolescent deviancy, it considerably added to the hole that appears likely to swallow the Youth Service up. The sort of solution that youth work could offer had little to do with the deeper structural and social changes that underpinned the panic. Thus, the performance of the Youth Service would or could then be measured against criteria over which it had fundamentally no control and little influence.

One way of rationalizing the moral panic approach and the lack of coherent thinking about philosophy and purpose has been the adoption of 'issue-based' approaches by some local youth services. In this they have been further encouraged by the way in which pockets of central government money can be obtained for particular pieces of work. Certain phenomenon such as unemployment, school non-attendance, drug abuse, racism and sexism are defined as an 'issue' and become the focus for resource allocation. This is sometimes accompanied by a shift from generalized person-centred rhetoric into that associated with the correct stance on the issue. The inherent dangers in this movement are threefold. First, as the shift is rarely based on coherent political analysis or even an adequate understanding of youth work, the result is often a riot of posturing, a few bright spots of practice and for the rest, business much as its usual muddled self. Many of the bright spots would have occurred anyway, for they are invariably the result of workers possessing a more substantial political understanding and identity (Jeffs and Smith, 1988b). Here the Women's and various black political movements have been of special significance in terms of workers' understandings and have been shown in more directed practice. Where attention has been paid to the relationship of the personal to the political, as is the case in much feminist practice, the work is also more likely to be person-centred. Keeping things at the level of 'issues' can mean that priorities remain informed by surface debates rather than by deeper political principles and realities. As a result, there is a tendency to treat issues as unique and separate, rather than springing from living within a particular social, economic and political system.

Secondly, treating racism or sexism as an 'issue' is particularly suspect. It can all too easily patronize, undermine and marginalize the efforts of those seeking to address fundamental ills. As Reeves and Chevannes have noted, 'in order to express their political aspirations, black students have had to form *parallel* organizations in their youth clubs, churches, associations and supplementary schools, thus contributing to their relative isolation from main-stream schooling activity' (1984: 182). The very existence of projects outside the formal sector that are engaged in the construction of a relevant education for black young people allows policy makers to slip away from tackling the fundamental problem of racism in the school and its curriculum. They can always argue that they are already doing something through the Youth Service or whatever. It is one thing to allow difficult or contested aspects of education in a marginal sector, quite another to face it in schools.

Thirdly, the adoption of issue-based approaches can actually weaken youth work because they do not play to its strengths. This will be dealt with at some length in Chapters 6 and 7. Here it is only necessary to note that in issue-based approaches there is often a resort to cultural aggression and imperialism, wherein workers attempt to gain acceptance for the correct position (as defined by them) rather than making the culture of those worked with the starting point. When placed in a class perspective it begins to look much like the child-saving of early youth workers, seeking to combat the 'nastiness' of working-class culture.

As a solution to the problem of purpose, defining particular matters as issues (and then directing resources at work which claims to offer some kind of solution) looks questionable. The fact that such approaches can be heralded as an advance is indicative both of the lack of thought given to essential purpose and the relative absence of any lasting tradition of analytical rigour within youth work.

Theory

Little sustained and critical attention has been devoted to the development of the craft of youth work. Many of the factors already identified as hampering front-line thinking about purpose apply generally to the state of theory-making within youth work. Furthermore, it has to be recognized that the reflectiveness of practitioners and trainers has remained largely rooted in one plane. This can be seen in the value that is placed upon experience within the work. At one level this can simply mean that people are not listened to if they themselves have not actually 'worked at the coalface'. 'Being there' is more important than 'understanding'. At another level it is sometimes expressed in the form that the only good theory is that which derives from experience, anything else can be dismissed as jargon. Thus, in training, students may be pushed to explore their feelings and practice and asked to develop theories that 'explains' things. This is fine in as far as it goes, but what can then happen is a failure to address questions and issues that established theories may pose, and the understandings students develop. In other words, the theoretical tools that are brought to bear are limited and the result is that there is not only a constant danger of reinventing the wheel, but also of never advancing theory and therefore practice. Youth work appears stuck in the realm of feelings, personal experience and immediate empirical perception. The non-theoretical cannot go beyond immediate appearances (Hall *et al.*, 1978: 52). To borrow from Gramsci, not only do youth workers have no precise consciousness of their historical identity, they are not even conscious of the historic identity or the exact limits of their adversaries (1971: 273).

Training agencies must take their share of the blame for this anti-intellectual and atheoretical current that runs through youth work. Here particular attention has to be paid to the work of the National College for the Training of Youth Leaders which was established following recommendations in the Albemarle Report (HMSO, 1960). It is significant for three main reasons. Firstly, its staff made a major contribution to the literature of youth work in the 1960s and early 1970s (Davies and Gibson, 1967; Leighton, 1972; Matthews, 1966). Secondly, following its closure in 1971, many of its staff were involved in the development of initial training courses in other higher education institutions. Not surprisingly, certain character-istics of the National College were reproduced in their respective courses. In addition, some of its staff went on to set up YSIC, the forerunner of the National Youth Bureau. Thirdly, just under 1100 people gained their qualification at the College during its 9.5 years of operation. A significant number of these students are now in officer, senior worker and training posts and thereby have an important influence upon the Service.

Ewen, in a much quoted commentary on the work of the College in the 1960s, argues that while it purported to have no particular slant, it was clear that the professional ethos that emerged included such attitudes as non-judgementalism, non-directiveness, accep-tance and so forth (1972: 6). Such an ethos all too easily deteriorates into an uncritical attitude to theory. Indeed, the emphasis in such training upon attitude can occur at direct cost to theory-making. As well as a concern with attitude and personal development, the major assumptions underlying the course were directed towards particular skill areas such as using activity and social group work (Watkins, 1972: 7–8). It is perhaps indicative of the College's attitude to established bodies of theory, that lectures were abolished in the late 1960s and increased reliance put on seminars (Watkins, 1972: 35).

Following the decision of the DES to do away with the 'narrowly based' National College (DES, 1969: 112) and to relocate youth work training, little of any theoretical consequence has appeared from trainers (Jeffs and Smith, 1987b). Further, an investigation of the various course documents submitted to CETYCW, reveals that, aside from the ritual addition of some discussion of the latest run of moral panics, the content of those elements of courses specifically devoted to developing an understanding of youth work is remarkably unchanged from the 1960s.

The overall emphasis on experience was underpinned by the strong influence upon Youth Service training of humanistic psychology in the guise of human awareness training and the like. Leigh and Smart comment that by the late 1970s many Youth Service trainers had gone overboard on the approaches suggested by such trainers as Pfeiffer and Jones (1969), Rogers (1967, 1969, 1973) and the various writers in the transactional analysis tradition:

in the excitement with which the Service embraced some

apparently powerful methods, it once again lost sight of purposes. In our experience, these 'person centred' approaches – with their typical emphasis on the realm of feelings and their characteristically non-directive, facilitative approach to issues of leadership – are widely employed whatever the subject matter. In the extreme any thinking or analysis is stigmatized as task-centred, and construed as evading the one true realm of feeling. (Leigh and Smart, 1985: 53)

This situation has been given a further twist by only a minority of the full-time youth work labour force being specialist trained. Kuper (1985) found that 43 per cent are qualified teachers, 17 per cent qualified by alternative routes, 13 per cent are unqualified and that only 27 per cent have received specialized training. While the make-up of the labour force would appear to indicate that a significant proportion of new entrants will have some grounding in education theory and the social sciences, the majority will not have had any sustained exposure to thinking about informal education. In addition, the fact that people gain their qualifications (and hence a significant part of their socialization as workers) in such different ways will not encourage the development of a shared language and occupational culture, and particularly of one that values analytical rigour. This position is further aggravated by the diverse and dispersed nature of youth work provision, where it is rare for full-time workers to work together in any substantial way. What often occurs when they get together is a sharing of frustrations, rather than deep attention to purpose and practice.

Problematic as it is, the position could have altered in some way if the various national agencies in youth work had paid attention to the state of youth work theory and to the sorts of research required. Unfortunately, a key body such as NYB became enmeshed in a peculiar mix of advocacy and servicing, based upon funding which directed attention away from the heartland of Youth Service activity and into the arenas of intermediate treatment, youth action, unemployment projects and youth counselling. While there may have been some important contributions to the work of these individual areas (Adams *et al.*, 1981; Lawton 1984; Burley 1980), the only substantial direct additions to the general discourse of youth work have been made in the form of a number of research papers by D.I. Smith (1979, 1980, 1985), the research undertaken by Butters and Newell (1978), and the work associated with the Panel to Promote the Continuing Development of Training for Part-time and

Voluntary Youth and Community Workers (Bolger and Scott, 1984; Harper, 1983, 1985). In comparison with a body such as the National Children's Bureau, this is a very sorry record.

Other national agencies have done little better. In terms of writing about, and encouraging the development of 'good practice', only one agency, NAYC, stands out in the 1970s and early 1980s as making a direct contribution on any scale. However, much of this work has only made a limited addition to theory and is derived from limited-term project work. The major source of sustained reflection upon practice was the *Working with Girls Newsletter*, which NAYC shoddily closed in a cost-cutting exercise in 1987. Most of the other initiatives and developments have come from organizations and groupings outside the national framework such as the Youth Development Trust and *Youth and Policy*, or from academics outside initial training. In the case of the latter grouping, the balance of the contribution here has been towards a historical and socio-logical understanding of the area and to questions of policy.

In short, theorizing about the purpose and practice of youth work is highly deficient. The key institutions that could have been expected to make a significant contribution in this area, have largely failed to make thinking a priority. As a result, there is not an adequate body of knowledge to help workers, officers and trainers to name, predict and act. This is clearly demonstrated by the parlous state of thinking concerning the supposed centre of youth work – social education (see Chapter 5).

The demise of the Youth Service?

Overall, the position looks bleak for the Youth Service. While there may be occasional peaks of optimism, perhaps as a minister throws the Service a few pennies as a means of demonstrating the government's commitment to 'solving' some political problem, the underlying trends suggest its demise. From what has been argued here and elsewhere (Jeffs and Smith, 1987b, 1988a), the intellectual, organizational and political basis for the Youth Service looks distinctly shaky. The broad attack on the idea of welfare, moves towards privatization, the lack of government priority given to youth, the massive expansion of parallel provision, and the failure to develop the thinking necessary to further the craft of youth work, leave the Youth Service and significant elements of practice in a perilous position. This is further aggravated by the relatively stronger intellectual, institutional and practical bases of much parallel provision. These trends in youth policy indicate that the government sees the Youth Service as marginal to their central concern to 'skill' the youth population and to secure their allegiance. They would appear to suggest a withering away of a distinctive statutory service.

The development or continuance of youth work within schooling, further education, leisure, social work, and within those settings concerned with counselling and advice appears likely. Within these areas the uncertainties concerning purpose and theory have, to some extent, been alleviated where practitioners have reinterpreted the different traditions of practice in order to fit the institutions where they are placed. Many of the 'new' tasks that it is suggested youth workers may undertake, e.g. around school and YTS drop-outs, can easily be approached from institutional bases other than the Youth Service. Even the government's somewhat belated interest in inner-city youth following the 1987 election can apparently be accommodated in leisure departments and community and further education sections. In many respects youth work appears to be set for the sort of locational diversity that community work has experienced.

What may remain as a distinctive 'youth' entity is some facility that governments and local authorities can use in order to be seen to be doing something about particular moral panics. Clearly, the State will continue to respond to such panics and will require some means of expressing their 'concern' and perhaps even of doing something about the 'problem'. Organizationally it is not necessary to have a department of 'moral panics', but the responses are usually required to adopt a reasonably high profile. For this reason local authorities sometimes choose to set up special committees or commissions to deal with issues, often of an inter-departmental nature. In some authorities, the Youth Service may live on in the form of a coordinating committee to deal with the successive waves of moral panics associated with youth. There may even be a future for detached 'action-researchers' in order that the committee deliberations may be informed.

What of the future for voluntary youth organizations? First, those organizations with a strong identity and clear ideology are likely to develop, although not necessarily grow. For as long as there exists within any social movement a clear rationale for work with young people, then it is likely that such work will carry on. Thus certain churches will continue to see that they have a mission concerning young people and political movements will similarly wish to get their message across and gain converts. However, when we turn to examine some of the youth organizations that are movements in themselves, such as Scouting and Guiding, then some questions do remain. Within these movements there has been some discussion as to their distinctive contribution and the extent to which this has changed since their inception. In particular, within Scouting, there appears to have been a shift away from more full-blown notions of improvement into a concern with healthy enjoyment. However, this debate has remained within the traditions of character-building. The fact that there is a coherent and common tradition within the work, combined with a clearly structured and common series of programme options and rules, does mean that questions of identity and ideology are less problematic than within other organizations which have adopted more generic programmes such as the YMCA.

National youth organizations with a clear identity and structure, and those organizations firmly rooted in social movements (with the exception of the Boys' Clubs), have only ever made passing reference to the idea of a Youth Service and, in terms of day-to-day operation, make very little use of the services offered by local authority Youth Services. They usually have their own training systems, a full range of local, regional and national activities, financial arrangements that call for little state funding (other than subsidized use of school halls and the like), and recruitment, both of workers and young people, through their own networks. In addition, their political power is usually exercised outside the Youth Service. For these reasons, while there may be some ritual mourning of the passing of LEA Youth Services, such organizations will hardly notice their disappearance.

Secondly, there would appear to be a future for the local or neighbourhood club or group, run by volunteers or part-timers, which aims to provide a safe, social and communal environment for young people. While in some areas this may be threatened by the development of commercial provision, a number of factors would appear to indicate its continued health. One of the central features is its 'local' nature, which means that provision is both close to home and is identified with the locality. This, combined with the presence of workers from the same area, and who are often connected with local community organizations such as religious groups and village and tenants halls, can make for some sense of belonging to a community, which is valued. That sense of community is further enhanced where there is a shared culture and a distinctively Greek, Bangladeshi or 'mining' club or group can emerge. In addition, such provision is often small-scale and cheap. Finally, notions of safety are also important in the minds of many parents and young people when choosing how to spend their leisure time. Localized provision, run by people or organizations known in the community and whose scale and nature makes for a fair degree of interaction between workers and young people, will remain an attractive option.

Such local groups have historically made rather more use of their Youth Service than have the movement-based organizations. A number of authorities have, in effect, recognized the significance of localized small-scale provision in the deployment and location of youth workers. Of some significance here is the withdrawal of workers from sustained face-to-face work with young people into so called 'area' or 'support' roles, where their task is to maintain and improve the services offered by voluntary groups or smaller units. However, from the perspective of the policy-maker, there is not any particular reason why such servicing should be the prerogative of a separate youth service. Depending upon how a particular authority labels such work it could easily be housed within a leisure, community education, social service or community work section.

What all this adds up to is further diversification and speciali-zation. Certainly youth work associated with schooling and FE looks likely to continue, as does that located within personal social services and leisure provision. The future for certain other forms of provision looks especially rocky. In particular, it would appear that larger youth centres and clubs, with one or more full-time youth workers, are often not attracting young people on a substantial enough scale to informal sessions to resist pressure from policy-makers for more cost-effective provision. Even where large numbers are attracted to more formal activities, these could frequently be run without the day-to-day attention of full-time workers. In this respect the health and potential of communally organized leisure provision such as that associated with sport, hobbies, arts and crafts is beginning to attract policy-makers' attention (Bishop and Hoggett, 1986: 123). The relative shift into small-scale convivial provision or larger-scale or more specialized leisure provision looks set to continue. From the evidence presented, the rationale for a distinctive, educationally-based, Youth Service is now increasingly seen by policy makers as rather weak. Other provision can seemingly offer what the Youth Service promised in 1960, but has failed to deliver since.

If the Youth Service faces its demise, what is the future for youth work? The remainder of this book suggests how we can move beyond current practice to develop a popular youth work based on informal education and mutual aid.

Chapter 5

Beyond Social Education

In the mid-1980s there was talk of the 'emerging crisis of purpose in social education' (Leigh and Smart, 1985). Whether or not this crisis of purpose only then appeared is debatable. What is certain is that social education has been used as an expression of purpose and method by many within youth work, yet it is rarely subjected to serious enquiry. While some attempts have been made to breathe life into the concept (NIYWA, 1987), social education is not visible in a sustained and consistent body of practice. At the same time, the term has been increasingly used within schooling. Many of the confusions and tensions concerning its usage within youth work are also present there.

Youth workers and officers are subject to a range of pressures from both outside and within the occupation, concerning their professional identity. Social education has been a key means of explaining their job both to themselves and to others. At first glance the notion does appear to describe the occupation – the use of social activities for educational ends. The 'social' is usually invested with a double meaning, one relating to method and the other to content. In the case of the latter, social education is generally used to refer to the personal development of the individual, particularly in relation to others. Hence the Albemarle Report was able to say:

> To encourage young people to come together into groups of their own choosing is the fundamental task of the Service. Their social needs must be met before their needs for training and formal instruction. . . . It means too, that it is the task of the Service to offer, in its own different environment, social education of the kind that has long been valued in the corpor-

ate life of those pursuing formal education in schools, technical colleges and universities. (HMSO, 1960: 52)

Not surprisingly, social education has been used to describe a wide variety of activities – some educational, many not. It has become little more than a rhetorical device. 'The variety of meanings attached to this term often succeed only in hindering its usefulness as a helpful concept' (ILEA, 1986: 3). Further, as a partial result of its role in 'explaining' the work, social education has often been treated as if it was youth work's 'property', its own invention, yet its roots lay somewhere quite different.

A history of social education

Social education entered the vocabulary of US educationalists by the late 1890s and there was even a quarterly journal devoted to its study. By 1908 Scott was advocating it as a contribution towards a 'more comprehensive and deeper social synthesis organically united with a freer and more thorough-going individual development' (Scott, 1908: v). 'The individual must learn that he is to be held responsible for his acts. . . . He must feel that either singly or in combination with others he is the cause of what happens' (1908: 281). Scott placed an emphasis on education for democratic citizenship. Crucially, he recognized the pedagogic implications and advocated a self-organized approach to group work. This portrayed the school as a social organism that could be used for developing cooperative attitudes and competencies. 'Liberty can only be realized by conduct, and its expression is always self-direction, self-organization, and self-control' (1908: 13).

In contrast, within British youth work, Baker makes early and explicit use of the concept in a rather pedestrian way: 'the Social Agencies not only interest and amuse a boy, but under good leadership, they smooth his rough edges and impart to him a polish' (1919: 130). This 'polish' was apparently to include being taught:

to take off his hat upon entering the Department; to say 'please' and 'thank you', and to be civil; not to be impertinent; to mind his own business and refrain from personal comment. Opportunities will be found for showing him that chivalrous respect is due to womanhood. Cleanliness of person and apparel, and in a hundred other details can be encouraged in an unobtrusive way. (Baker, 1919: 130)

Booton (1985) suggests that the concept was also in use within the

Charity Organizations Society at this time. However, the concern appears to go beyond the question of manners, having:

> more of a literal meaning indicating the individual's *education* (ie knowledge, understanding) about society and social processes. As such it did not denote a particular curriculum, much less a specific practice, and was probably directed as part of the typical reformist language mainly towards middle class adults. (Booton, 1985: 10)

It was a concern which was present in the interest in citizenship by educationalists in the 1930s and in social studies in the late 1940s (M. Smith, 1987: 10–12). Significantly, the advocacy of a broadly-based social studies was linked to an emphasis upon active learning and a challenge to the traditional organization of the secondary school curriculum. Somewhat idealistically, Hemming saw one of the aims as the fostering of:

> the development of spontaneity, self reliance, flexibility of mind, clear thinking, tolerance, initiative, articulateness, adventurousness of outlook, courage in the face of new problems, enjoyment of created activity, sound standards of action and appreciation, world-mindedness, a sense of purpose and philosophy of life. (Hemming, 1949: 8)

In these early representations we can see many of the strands present in current usage. However, within youth work it is the Albemarle Report which is usually taken as the landmark in the usage of the term. It asserted that the Youth Service provided for 'continued social and informal education of young people in terms most likely to bring them to maturity, that of responsible personal choice' (HMSO, 1960: 103). Certainly by the mid-1960s there began to be a more widespread use of the phrase. For instance, Evans (1965) includes a chapter entitled 'Social Education' which discusses briefly youth work's contribution to the social development of young people. Significantly, nowhere in this chapter does Evans mention social education or interpret it. This was left to Davies and Gibson (1967), who defined the term around the idea of maturity, and developed an analysis of the practice and institutions that must accompany it. The prime concern was 'with any young person's meetings with others, with his capacity in these meetings to accept others and be accepted by them, and the ideas, thoughts and opinions, the motives and the emotions inherent in such meetings and interests' (Davies and Gibson, 1967: 12). Its product was:

> any individual's increased consciousness of himself – of his

values, aptitudes and untapped resources and of the relevance of these to others. It enhances the individual's understanding of how to form mutually satisfying relationships, and so involves a search for the adult for ways of helping a young person to discover how to contribute to as well as take from his associations with others. (Davies and Gibson, 1967: 12)

This demands young people's involvement in relevant situations and interrelationships – the process cannot be detached as an exclusively intellectual exercise. Davies and Gibson emphasized social education as a particular type of process directed at a specific task – the social development of adolescents. Here education (and learning) were seen as gerund – words which can be used as a noun or a verb. Learning can, therefore, be viewed as either an internal change in consciousness or as the process of acquiring knowledge, feelings and skills. In this context, then, social education is a particular type of learning process and/or an attempt to achieve an internal change of consciousness such as the achievement of maturity (in what ever way that is defined). The importance of this was that it conceptualized and symbolized a shift from an emphasis in youth work debates from personal adjustment to person-centredness. For those committed to personal adjustment, 'society's' rules and norms would be taken as given and young people adjusted to this view of maturity. In contrast, the new social education focused rather more on the process of learning and, hence, upon the relationship of the worker/teacher to the person.

There is a further possible characteristic hinted at in all this, that of setting or context. Social education may, thus, be defined by the context or setting in which a process or task is situated. It is 'in society'. A crude expression of this view is the way in which the school is sometimes set against the 'community' as a site for learning. Thus, social education might occur when young people are given opportunities to learn within the community such as in programmes of voluntary or community involvement. While this is a rather narrow view, the emphasis upon community involvement, as against personal development or the more embracing concern with the relationship of the self, others and society (Elliot and Pring, 1975: 9), does reveal a further, important strand of practice. For example, the Schools Council Social Education Project saw as its final goal the promotion in young people of an active interest in the affairs of their community (Rennie *et al.*, 1974: 130). This was to be achieved by providing 'an enabling process through which children will achieve a sense of identification with their community, become sensitive to its

shortcomings and develop methods of participation in those activities needed for the solution of social problems' (Rennie *et al.*, 1974:
130). Earlier, in a similar vein, the Fairbairn-Milson Report asserted
that social education was the primary goal of youth work:

> We are not so much concerned today as in the past with basic
> education, or with economic needs, or with the communica-
> tion of an agreed value system; but we are concerned to help
> young people to create their place in a changing society and it is
> their critical involvement in their community which is the goal.
> (DES 1969: 55)

> Our commitment is to a society in which every member can be
> publicly active. . . . We seek the 'active society' in which all
> are encouraged and enabled to find the public expression of
> their values, avoiding the extremes of indifference and aliena-
> tion . . . all individuals should grow towards maturity. (DES,
> 1969: 59–60)

In the context of the current emphasis upon vocationalism and
leisure, these social democratic sentiments evoke nostalgia, much
like bowling alleys, Biba clothes and Ford Anglias. Not surprisingly,
they were not translated into a widespread body of practice.

During the late 1970s and the 1980s, there was a renewal of interest in social education within the more formalized arenas of education and training but not within youth work. In part, attention to
social education has been occasioned by the arrival of YOP and YTS
and the organization of curriculum elements around the notion of
'social and life skills' (Further Education Unit, 1980; Hopson and
Scally, 1981). Further, the advocacy of political education and of the
importance of improving young people's political literacy once
again drew attention to aspects of a possible social education
curriculum (Crick and Porter, 1978). The introduction of programmes such as Active Tutorial Work (Baldwin and Wells,
1979–81) and Group Tutoring (Button, 1981, 1982) into schools may
well have increased interest alongside more academic investigation
(David, 1983; Pring, 1984; Brown *et al.*, 1986). Recent discussion
has addressed both process and content. In her survey of the area Lee
suggests that social education can be used to cover:

> all those teaching or informal activities which are planned by
> curriculum developers, teachers or other professionals to
> enhance the development of one or more of the following:
>
> knowledge, understanding, attitudes, sensitivities, com-
> petence, in relation to:

- the self and others, and/or
- social institutions, structures and organizations and/or
- social issues. (Lee, 1980: 5)

Such a definition allows social education to subsume what has been described as 'social and life skills'. It has the merit of focusing attention upon the different ways in which the curriculum is constructed and of recognizing that some teachers and workers may work in all three areas, while others may concentrate on one or two. On the other hand, it restricts usage to professionalized interventions as against the conscious attempts by, say, parents or peers, to further the social and personal development of others.

A number of contributions have also emphasized the importance of pedagogy (BYV Social Education Project, 1981; Scottish Community Education Centre, 1982). As Brown *et al.* comment, 'it may be that the best practice in social education is not expressed through a curriculum at all but through the quality of the learning situations created throughout the curriculum as a whole and the relationships which pervade the entire school' (1986: 11). Such an interest in process has, to some extent, characterized the few written discussions of social education in youth work that have appeared since the 1970s (M. Smith, 1980, 1982; Burley, 1982; Booton, 1985). Here the concern has been to emphasize cooperative and collective means of working, the focus upon the person, the importance and means of recognizing and harnessing people's experiences, the significance of problem-posing, and the necessity of placing such processes in a political perspective.

Underlying the various shifts that have occurred in the theory and practice of social education are a number of assumptions that have a direct bearing upon the usefulness of the idea for practitioners. Three themes are of particular significance:

(i)   There are questions about the way social education in youth work has been conceptualized around youth, or rather adolescence and the dangers inherent in notions such as 'growing-up' and maturity.

(ii) Social educational practice has been dominated by a focus on the individual and small group and a lack of attention to the political nature of practice.

(iii) The way in which the self has been conceptualized can lead to the charge of ethnocentrism (and sexism, as we have already seen in Chapter 1).

Growing up

Every society is faced with the problem of how to ensure that successive generations are socialized into ways of thinking and behaving which serve the community or the needs of particular groups within it. This process is open to eternal debate and the sort of answers given will depend, to a large extent, on the position occupied within that community. For the individual there is the problem of making the transition from some state known as childhood to another known as adulthood, between or overlapping which there is something known as youth or adolescence. Within these states there appear to be differing expectations concerning dependency and responsibility. One way of conceptualizing the transition is to see it as a movement from relationships characterized by a high degree of dependency to ones which contain a greater degree of independence. Thus, young children are initially dependent on older family members for the most part for the satisfaction of their needs. As they grow older in Western societies, they move outside their family, first at school and in the peer groups they join, then perhaps through further education, training or work. At some point they are likely to leave the family and set up a household of their 'own'. Another, and related, way of viewing the transition is to think in terms of changing responsibilities both for oneself and for others. Youth is therefore a period when more and more responsibilities are taken on. This position is reflected in legal terms by the differing ages at which people are seen as being able to take responsibility for their actions.

People make this transition at different rates and in different ways. Age is only one factor in determining experiences. Class, geographical location, gender, ethnicity and physical and mental 'ability' all can have a major bearing (Jeffs and Smith, 1988b). In many societies transitions may be marked by explicit rituals or 'rites of passage', e.g. birth, naming children, attaining adulthood, marriage and death. Thus, initiation rituals remove people from the status of child and place upon them the new position of 'marriageable adult'. To mark this fundamental transition, both psychologically and socially:

> the novice is first physically separated from, and systematically divested of, his old position as child. He has ritually to put away childish things, and is frequently spirited off to a conditioning camp in the wilderness, that inexhaustible fount of

mystical energy and renewal. There he is symbolically stripped of his old personality and enters a transitory limbo. Finally purged of his old social personality, the new recruit is eased into his new position in adult society with an appropriate ritual accompaniment. (Lewis, 1976: 131).

Within industrialized societies the rituals and symbols of transition are less marked or, rather, do not play such a powerful role in communal life. Further, the length of the transitory limbo has grown. Hence, in Chapter 1, we saw how specifically male and female conceptions of adolescence came to be constructed. Adolescence was also shown to be the product of particular circumstances at a specific moment of history and not a universal condition. While there may have been some conception of 'youth' and even a period of transition, what Victorian middle-class social reformers wanted to impose on young people was new in many respects. This was a period of enforced and extended dependence on adults, not just a symbolic moment of transition. It was a time which had to be traversed in order that maturity may be achieved. The way in which such thinking has been reflected in the theory and practice of youth work can be seen to disadvantage young people in a number of respects.

First there is the ever-present tendency to undervalue people as they are now. In Milson's memorable phrase, young people must be valued as human beings, for what they are now, not only for what they may become (Milson, 1970: 85). It is all too easy to look at behaviours that are labelled 'temporary' or the 'excesses of youth' and fail to understand how real they are to those that are experiencing them or, indeed, to recognize their inherent value and importance. This is not restricted to youth. If workers are seeking to achieve any sort of change in people then there is a danger of undervaluing people as they are: both denying the expertise and competencies that they already possess, and the logic of their behaviour and ideas at that moment.

Secondly, the association of particular types of behaviour with age has contributed to a paternalism and a growing dependency. Clearly, there has been a significant increase in the length of time that young people remain dependent upon their family for shelter, food and disposable income since the mid-nineteenth century. This has been combined with a growing uniformity in the timing of major life transitions. Thus, young people have been able to be more precise in their age expectations. At the same time the status associated with 'growing up', the movement away from dependency, has meant that the next stage is highly aspirational for young people, but in many adults' eyes progress towards it has to be slow. As Macleod has commented in the context of early work on boys in the US, this has profound implications for practice:

> Programs would have been unthinkable without a consti-tuency of dependent adolescents in need of recreation; yet the boys' sensitivity to age differences made them hard to hold. Pervasive age grading had reoriented the issue between adults and boys; instead of a few convulsive struggles for autonomy, there were endless little tests along a finely calibrated course. The boys wanted more tokens of maturity, yet had no inten-tion of demanding total independence. Adults wanted to hold the boys back but not to cripple their initiative. (Macleod 1983: 28)

The upshot of this is, that within youth work, age-related expecta-tions have contributed towards dependency in practice. There has been an emphasis on provision for young people rather than by them. Furthermore, a great deal of effort has been directed at seeking to restrain young people from progressing too fast to the next stage, e.g. in terms of sexual behaviour, drinking and unsupervised leisure. Much 'social education' has, therefore, been aimed at getting young people to appreciate and conform to age-related, rather than com-petency-related, definitions of acceptable behaviours.

Thirdly, the focus on youth as *the* period of transition can lead to a lopsided practice, as life itself is 'transitional'. Within the category 'adult' there are many moments of change. Parenthood, the impact of the ageing process, changes in relationships, the death of parents and friends, changes in work – all of these affect the way we see our-selves and the way that others see us. This is not to say that practi-tioners should not concern themselves with change, for patently they should, rather than plead for a sense of fluidity and criticism. Where social education is seen as synonymous with social and per-sonal development, it is difficult to sustain the case for linking its definition to particular age ranges.

Fourthly, there are real doubts about the nature of the transition stage, the state which is to be traversed. While the ideology of adolescence was applied to middle-class youth by early com-mentators with great success, on the whole, working-class traditions and cultures were far less easy to control and penetrate. Crucially, this failure to elicit the required response from working-class young people did not lead to the abandonment of the concept of adolescence:

Instead it was stretched to explain 'precociousness' and 'anti-social' forms of behaviour by reference to the incompetence of working class parents, who it was frequently claimed, failed to treat their children with the correct affectionate and authoritarian control during this traumatic stage in life. (Humphries, 1981: 18)

Much of the theory that has informed the use of the concept of adolescence within youth work, both psychological and sociological, has characterized it as a time of disturbance, storm and stress. As NAYC argued in its evidence to the Youth Service Review, this way of thinking about adolescence 'has been empirically unsound and as a consequence has been a considerable blockage to thinking about appropriate provision for young people' (National Association of Youth Clubs, 1981: 4). The reality is, of course, that the vast bulk of young people do not show signs of disturbance and, that those who do, form a proportion of the age range in line with both the child and adult population. The important difference being that, during this age period, problems tend to be of other types, with depression being the most prevalent. Thus, 'adolescence needs a theory, not of abnormality, but of normality' (Coleman, 1980: 182). It is not the intention here to argue that age is of no significance in understanding the experiences of young people – clearly it is. Certain patterns of physical, social and emotional development are associated with specific age bandings. As an explanatory idea it has to take its place alongside other variables such as class, sex, race, sexuality, location and disability. What is at issue here are some of the generalizations made about adolescence and the way these feed certain understandings of social education.

All this amounts to a powerful argument for approaching notions such as youth and adolescence with caution, for recognizing that they may well have meaning in terms of young people's experience, and for the reorientation of prescribed aims away from ideas such as maturity. In other words, practitioners need to view youth as a way of recognizing their target group, rather than as a problem to be traversed. Instead, if seeking to help young people 'grow up', a more appropriate course might be to respond to them in such a way as to allow them to take responsibility for their own learning and to face the consequences of that. It is, of course, highly likely that questions of age-related behaviours will be a central motif in the dialogue with young people. However, these behaviours need to be set alongside other factors such as class and gender, and will require practitioners to guard against responses which confirm dependency.

The problems of a personalist orientation

Much practice has remained rooted in the personal, without reference to broader forces that help structure life chances and experiences. This tendency was recognized by Montagu at the turn of the century:

> Like other philanthropists, club workers are all too easily satisfied with fringing the problems with which they should endeavour to grapple. They peep down into the abyss in which the under-fed, the ill-housed and badly clothed work out their life's drama, and then turn their energies to surface polishing. They try to make their girls conduct themselves well in the clubs and interest them and amuse them as best they can during their evening's leisure. But they are inclined to forget the grim truth that, if girls work for less than a living wage, in a vitiated atmosphere, they are not likely to become the strong, self-controlled women whom we desire the clubs to train. (Montagu, 1904: 249–50)

At one level this means that social educational practice in youth work rarely rises above the first of Lee's categories, that is beyond a concern with self and immediate others (1980:5). Sustained practice which addresses questions surrounding social institutions, structures and organizations, and social issues is thin on the ground. Yet the problem goes deeper than this, for the way in which the personal dimension is approached fails to appreciate that 'personal troubles cannot be solved merely as troubles, but must be understood in terms of public issues – and in terms of the problem of history making (Mills, 1970: 248). There are exceptions to this as the growth of feminist youth work practice has demonstrated. Spence (1988) argues that such practice begins with a recognition of the conditions and relationships within which young women live their lives and from which they construct their understanding of themselves, and that this involves relating to their actual material situation. However, the quality of work in this area still remains patchy.

Making the self and others the dominant focus could be excusable if the surface was disturbed and questions about agency and structure were made an integral part of practice. The relationship between individuals and social structure is a matter of some debate. We might begin with Marx's classic line 'Men make their own history, but they do not make it just as they please; they do not make it under circumstances chosen by themselves, but under circumstances directly encountered, given, and transmitted from the past' (1977b: 300). However, within this there are many questions. In what ways do structures determine what individuals do, how are those structures made and what limits are there then upon individuals to act as agents independently of the constraint of structures? These are questions fundamental to any educational endeavour and have to be approached not just as a preliminary to practice, but also as an integral part of working with people. In other words, it is not only necessary to come to some understanding of the relation of agency to structure before making interventions, the furthering of such understanding is also an essential educational aim.

Willis (1977) provides an insight into the complex relations of agency and structure. In his study of a small group of working-class young men's resistance to schooling he found that such opposition actually fed and encouraged their acceptance of the productive system. He recognized that people know a great deal about the environment of which they form a part and that some of that knowledge is tacit, while much is able to be verbalized. The 'lads' in his study were knowledgeable actors whose actions had unintended consequences. Thus, in the sense it is their own culture which most effectively prepares some working-class lads for the manual giving of their labour power, 'we may say that there is some element of self damnation in the taking on of subordinate roles in Western capitalism. However, this damnation is experienced paradoxically, as true learning, affirmation, appropriation, and as a form of resistance' (Willis, 1977: 3). In other words, constraint was shown to operate through the active involvement of the agents concerned, not as some force of which they are passive recipients (Giddens, 1984: 289). Social forces were seen to be acting through agents' reasons. Educational practice which fails to take account of this is severely disabling. A focus on the self is only legitimate when understood in the totality of social relations. Day-to-day routines and commonsense understandings carry in them both the stuff of action and of constraint. They cannot be taken for granted. Thus, a central function of any educational endeavour must be to help people place themselves in the world – to know what exists, what is of their own making and what is of other forces, and to know what is good and what is possible.

Ethnocentrism

The concept of self that informs much discussion about social education is distinctly Western and individualistic. This can be seen clearly when considering teaching about family relationships and obligations. Johnson sums up the Western, and in particular North American, position as follows:

> Children are socialized simultaneously to be obedient, to submit to rules which protect the rights of others, *and* to develop a progressive independence. Operationally, independence means being able gradually to assume responsibility for their own actions, and to exercise [internal] control over their actions. (Johnson, 1985: 123)

Throughout this training the desirability of 'becoming independent' is explicitly raised. This is contrasted with Japanese thought where 'the prerogative for some forms of life-long [infantile] dependency upon selected others is normatively supported' (Johnson, 1985: 124). The acknowledgement of interdependence in work, friendship and family relations is explicit, conscious and central to social life. In a similar fashion, the Hindu concept of self leads to a rather different understanding of the significance of being 'individual'. It begins with the concept of the 'real-self' or *ātman*, which may be contrasted with the lower empirical or material self, i.e. the experiential form of self involving thought, desires and sensations. The Hindu self is therefore that of a 'dividual' rather than an 'individual':

> What would be seen as self-inconsistency in a westerner is perfectly understandable given the idea that Hindus do not see their situational behaviour as a reflection of their true self, but as a reflection of a lesser entity. . . . When the Hindu traditions speak about an individual, it is not to analyse but to denigrate. (Marsella *et al.*, 1985: 14)

Thus, when a Hindu man is asked for his identity, 'he will give you his name, the name of his village, and his caste' (Bharati, 1985: 211). There is a Sanskrit formula which begins with lineage, family, house and ends with personal name. In this presentation, the empirical self comes last. This contrasts with many Europeans who will identify themselves primarily and immediately by their job or special skill:

> The western striving is toward the development of a solid well-functioning ego. The inner experience of self should be clearly delineated from the outside. The Hindu striving goes in the opposite direction – to achieve union with the immutable self, which is ultimately indistinguishable from deity and the totality of the universe. (Marsella *et al.*, 1985: 18)

This underlines the fundamental importance of addressing how patterns of socialization and family interaction, and the operation of symbols within different cultures affect people's self conception and their way of placing themselves in the world. It is simply not possible to approach say, Hindu experience, through the application of Western models of thought. What results does not make sense, worse still the culture may then be stigmatized as irrational or silly. Understanding can only be attained by attempting to enter different cultural systems of thought. This has particular significance for those who are consciously engaged in education. They have to be sensitive to different senses of self and to amend the direction and delivery of their work accordingly. It places a primary duty on the educator to listen and act in such a way as to remain true to people's developing sense of themselves and to guard against the imposition of models of thinking which are of the educator's making or ownership.

Rescue, reform or abandonment?

In the preceding discussion, most of the attention has been on practice which is educational in ethos and which is genuinely informed by some recognizable 'theory' of social education. However, the term has been used to cover a multitude of sins, both within schooling and youth work. At least questions concerning the personalist orientation of practice, the focus on maturity and the westernized understanding of the self can be responded to practically and intellectually. Whether it is possible to rescue social education from its chronic misuse in other respects and to develop appropriate forms of pedagogy under its aegis poses different problems.

At the beginning of the 1980s, rescue did appear possible to some. For example, in earlier work, I suggested a way of thinking about social education that centred around enabling people to meet their developmental needs (1980, 1982). It was defined in such a way as to make a break with some of the thinking in Davies and Gibson (1967). For instance, social education was pictured as a process through life, that was not tied to the attainment of some fixed state such as 'maturity', but to the process of development, that was concerned with both individual and collective growth, and that could be mutual and not linked to adults doing things for young people. Social education seemed to be a convenient vehicle for the encouragement of educational as against recreational provision, and for the development of practice which accorded young people respect and power. Now a rather different judgement must be made, at least for youth work.

First, the term continues to be used in a loose way and to embrace practices that could in no way be seen as educational. Within youth work it is frequently applied to learning that would have happened anyway. Often provision entails activity for activity's sake without there being any specifically educational intent. In this way, the phrase has burrowed so deep into the youth work vocabulary, and it has become so corrupted and misused as to mean that any attempt at rescue or rediscovery is doomed. Once an idea becomes a rhetorical device and is applied indiscriminately, it ends up like the boy who cried wolf. No one believes that there is any substance to what is said. In many respects, the fact that the Youth Service Review (HMSO, 1982) was only able to discuss the term in a superficial manner, was the final symbolic nail in the coffin. The Review Report proclaimed that the Youth Service's task is to provide social education (HMSO, 1982: 122), yet nowhere is there any serious effort to actually define what is meant by this term. What we are told is that the processes by which youth work and work by other agencies assist personal development constitute a young person's social education (HMSO, 1982: 13), and that the Youth Service has developed specific methods of working, including the experiential curriculum, voluntaryism, a non-authoritative relationship between workers and young people, and encouraging young people to participate in decision making (HMSO, 1982: 34). Nowhere are these elements brought together in any coherent form. Social education is supposed to be youth work's central task, but a major report on the Service is unable to state clearly what it actually is.

Secondly, there has been a general association of social education with specific groups of young people and with 'low status' activities. The extent of this linkage means that it is difficult to see how the term can be reclaimed for universal work. In some schools social education may entail:

> little more than short courses in careers education or health education. Other courses are more elaborate and may incorporate . . . other topics such as moral education and political education. Alongside these courses, but not integrated with them, are likely to be courses in child care and parentcraft which have sprung up as an extension of home economics for the 'less able'. Even more elaboration is usually indicated when titles like 'social education', 'social studies' or 'community studies' are used. (C. Brown 1986: 8)

Such studies often appear in the fourth and fifth years of secondary schooling and their teachers frequently experience difficulties as what is taught does not fit into the usual range of examination-orientated subject divisions. The fact that social education is not examined, is seen to be non-academic, lacks resources and is often staffed by a rag bag of teachers from other subject areas means that it is viewed as peripheral and low-grade by young people, their parents and by the staff themselves. In addition, the association of the area with 'less able' students can lead to a deficit model, wherein those apparently lacking in particular skills or capacities are socially educated, while those possessing the appropriate social capital carry on with academic study. Similar 'streaming' can also occur within youth work. It is also significant that a number of adult training centres have been redesignated as social education centres (Blackburn, 1988). In addition, many of the activities are also seen to be high risk and 'controversial'. Sex education, peace education and political education can all excite fears of what response governors, parents or local politicians might make. This reputation of social education as a high risk/low status area has important implications when considering the relationship of youth workers to mainstream education. Their espoused specialism is viewed as troublesome, marginal and apparently capable of being undertaken by almost any teacher.

Thirdly, when we come to examine the two central elements that are commonly used to define the phenomenon, it is difficult to see that there is anything unique or specifically the property of social education. If we consider social education as an attempt to promote an internal change of consciousness, then it is usually so widely defined that the 'social' could be dropped. In other words, what we are concerned with is education. There cannot be much that in some way or form does not contribute to one's understanding of self, the relationship with others and with society as a whole. To a very real degree the use of phrases such as these are boundaryless. Where does social education end and other forms of education or other enterprises begin?

Concerns with the personal and the social transcend 'subject' barriers. It can be argued, for example, that all school subjects contribute to social and personal development in some measure. Indeed, if they did not, it would be difficult to see how they could be conceived of as educational. If the school or youth work unit is to be effective, then what is required is 'a careful, philosophical reflection upon what it means to be a person, how development as a person is inextricably linked with a form of social life, and where moral values and ideas are presupposed in both' (Pring, 1984: 167). The whole curriculum would then be interrogated for its contribution to people's development and in schools there would be no specially designated subject slot for 'social education' or the like. Against this last proposal, the pragmatist might ask 'why not?' If something is to be valued within the schooling system it has to have separate subject status. Furthermore, given that it touches upon personal values and sensitivities 'should it not logically be a matter for both experts and expert treatment?' (McBeath, 1986: 44). In this view something called 'social education' or 'social and personal development' can be recognized by the extent to which an emphasis is placed upon 'the immediate present and the immediate future of the self and self–other relationships' (McBeath, 1986: 43). Within the schooling sector there may well be an argument for this line of approach, where the case has to be put alongside a number of other curriculum demands. However, this is a restricted understanding of social education – again only covering the first of Lee's (1980) categories, and it still leaves crucial boundary problems.

Another answer to the boundary question is to alter the constraints on what 'social' is taken to mean. Here we might turn to the use of the term 'social education' in the USA, where there has remained a major strand of practice that links it with what might be called citizenship or political education. In other words, the 'social' is seen as societal and more specifically as enabling people to be active citizens (see, e.g. Morrissett and Williams, 1981). As those familiar with the debates within political education will already know, there are also problems in defining this activity's boundaries, but they are perhaps less problematic than those associated with social education (M. Smith, 1987). However, to redefine social education in this way in the UK would be a difficult task and would entail a major shift of focus. Another, pragmatic course of action is simply to assert that certain subject or topic areas such as careers and health studies, are social education. But this would be little more than playing with labels.

Turning to the conceptualization of social education as a particular type of process we can see similar problems arising. Social educators cannot claim property rights over group work, experiential learning or any of the other means that are employed. Indeed, such approaches are increasingly being used in other areas of the school curriculum. 'What makes for good social education is the same as what makes for good subject teaching. In other words, exploiting the dynamics and relations of the social group' (McBeath, 1986: 53). In schooling and youth work, there is not a particular method which can be labelled social education. This in itself, would not be a problem, if when method was joined with content, something unique and definable appeared. In reality what we find is an extraordinary range of concerns and practices, the only link between the many parts being that the term social education has been applied to them.

The mistake I made in earlier discussions of youth work was to assume that the scale and quality of genuinely developmental endeavour could be enhanced by directing practitioners' attention to the 'education' in 'social education'. My intention had been to emphasize ethos and method. However, the particular amalgam that emerged, in part because it was linked to an unreformable rhetorical device, was not a very effective tool in the attempt to encourage practitioners to see and understand themselves as educators, and to develop their competencies as such. A further limitation is that while a number of practitioners may conceive themselves as educators, the particular focus for purpose – personal and social development – is not one that a significant number see or experience as central to their work. A more effective course is to demarcate clearly purpose and method; to start from first principles and establish purpose and method while taking into account what youth work can offer as unique.

All this would suggest that the definitional and strategic problems associated with social education in youth work are of such a magnitude as to make the term useless as a theoretical, and hence practical tool. If those concerned with youth work perceive their endeavours as essentially educational, then to simply name them as such would appear to be a more profitable course of action. Historically youth workers have turned to the use of social facilities in order that educational or other work might happen. It was the linking of these two notions which perhaps accounts for the appeal of social education within youth work. Unfortunately, the act of joining together the words 'social' and 'educational', does not make a theory, nor a practice. Thus, it is not only a 'crisis of purpose' (Leigh and Smart, 1985), with which youth workers are faced. Social education has come to resemble another 'child' of the 1960s, system-built housing. Initially attractive and offering the promise of better times, it only takes a short while for paint to peel and for the inherent structural faults to blight the lives of residents. Often the only way to put right the problems is to demolish the whole structure and start again.

Chapter 6

Good Purpose

In this chapter we approach an apparently simple question, 'what should youth workers set out to do?' As with all such questions, searching for an answer is far from straightforward. The traditions discussed in Chapter 3 reveal a range of ideas about what the proper purpose of youth work might be. Such divergence is inevitable given the various interests involved. Again, there are debates as to the actual functions of youth work. Does it promote the welfare of individuals, serve to secure the reproduction of the means of production and existing power relations, promote community or what? Those questions have already been approached. Here our primary interest is in what should, and what could, be.

What is right? What is good?

Such is the variety of possible ends, values and ideals which are relevant to how individuals ought to live their lives and how a community ought to organize, that the problem is how to choose between them and implement programmes that realize their promise. In order to make choices we might ask what action is right or what action makes for the greatest good. The latter question expresses, of course, a utilitarian concern. The basic thesis is that whatever choice or policy maximizes the positive balance of pleasure over pain across a group, or for a single individual if only s/he is concerned, is what is good. There is a simple equation between 'the good' and happiness or pleasure. In so far as an action results in a good result, it is right. However, pleasure provides a less than adequate account of the good. It is not the sole good. Hence, within welfare economics in particular, an attempt has been made to replace the maximization of pleasure with the maximum satisfaction of desires or wants in predicted or actual preferences. In other words, we make a decision as to what might produce the greatest amount of utility. Thus, when appraising different programme possibilities, we ask what action maximizes benefits and minimizes costs for the whole group? There is an immediate problem in this. It can be argued that the principle of maximizing utility is incapable of protecting the fundamental interests of some individuals. 'Because the disadvantages to the few can be counter-balanced by benefits to the many, utilitarianism cannot justify a concern for basic individual interests' (Weale, 1983: 17). In this way it is possible that minorities can be severely disadvantaged.

Several alternatives to utilitarianism have been advanced, but the most influential in terms of recent social policy thinking has been the work of Rawls (1972). The central place he accorded to social justice provided a lift to those who believed that this was the proper aim of social policy. Rawls sought to construct an independent theory of justice. What is right or just was to be established separately from what is good or makes for the most good. He called his approach a *procedural* theory of justice: 'Pure procedural justice obtains when there is no independent criterion for the right result; instead there is a correct or fair procedure such that the outcome is likewise correct or fair, whatever it is' (Rawls, 1972: 86). The operational principles of justice are first that:

> each person is to have an equal right to the most extensive total system of equal basic liberties compatible with a similar system of liberty for all . . . [and, secondly, that] . . . social and economic inequalities are to be arranged so that they are both a) to the greatest benefit of the least advantaged, consistent with the just savings principle, and b) attached to offices and positions open to all under conditions of equality of opportunity. (Rawls, 1972: 302–3)

Rawls is, in essence, proposing three different concepts, ranked in this order:

(i) equality in basic liberties;
(ii) equality of opportunity for advancement;
(iii) positive discrimination in favour of the underprivileged to ensure equity. (Jones *et al.*, 1983: 14)

The argument is, that if such principles are followed, the outcome will necessarily be just and good, even though the exact experience of the just society cannot be specified in advance. However, in calling his theory of justice 'procedural', 'Rawls seems to bestow on it an aura of impartiality, whereas the procedures he specifies are designed to further a particular form of society' (Goodwin, 1982: 273). This form is implicit in the original assumptions. In other words, he smuggles a range of liberal ideas into what is claimed to be an objective theory. Thus, just how successful Rawls was in his enterprise, indeed whether his scheme is essentially different to utilitarianism, is open to considerable debate. In reality, his theory of fairness asserts a particular social idea without a substantial theory of the good.

In many respects Marx's account of the good poses similar problems. In his *Critique of the Gotha Programme*, Marx sets out some elements of the communist society:

> When the enslaving subordination of the individual to the division of labour, and with it the antithesis between mental and physical labour, has vanished; when labour is no longer merely a means of life but has become life's principle need; when the productive forces have also increased with the all-round development of the individual, and all the springs of co-operative wealth flow more abundantly – only then will it be possible to transcend the narrow outlook of bourgeois right, and only then will society be able to inscribe on its banners: From each according to his ability, to each according to his needs! (Marx, 1875: 263)

The socialist principle of distribution, while clearly exhibiting its value base, is also procedural. There is a clear ordering of criteria, with that of need being dominant in the distribution of material goods, and opportunities appropriate to talents, given that equal needs and talents are treated equally. 'Equality would be invoked in the many areas of life where need is not paramount. . . . Thirdly, merit may determine the distribution of any surplus goods when basic needs are satisfied' (Goodwin, 1982: 274). However, when we come to examine the nature of the communist society, we can see that Marx's notion of what is good for human beings centres around creative social labour. This is somewhat limited, especially when we consider other possible and additional candidates such as health, friendship, sex and religion.

In order to proceed further in our understanding of what the purpose of youth work should be, it is necessary to have both a more adequate theory of the good and a theory of justice and principles by which the good may be distributed. Such an original task is clearly beyond the scope of this book. Instead, we will follow a naturalist

line of analysis developed by Alan Brown (1986) and revert to an
Aristotlean argument. This is, that by identifying human nature in
sufficient detail, we shall discover to a reasonably determinate
extent the nature of human good. This is a similar exercise to that
suggested by Pring (1984) in respect of personal and social education
(see Chapter 5). He argued that such philosophical reflection 'should
be a part of the professional job of those who introduce personal and
social education into the curriculum and into the life of the school'
(Pring, 1984: 167). There will be many reading these words who are
either unfamiliar with this approach or who are schooled in another
tradition of moral philosophy. Here I want to simply say that this is
the route with which I am most happy. It is possible to reach a similar
end-point via somewhat different lines of argument (see, e.g.
Lindley, 1986).

Central to Aristotle's efforts is the question 'What is the good life
for wo/man?' This human good or *eudaimonia* is sometimes translated as human flourishing or well-being, and has much in common
with Mill's concept of human happiness (Lindley, 1986: 104). Brown
suggests that there are certain activities and behaviours that are
characteristic of humans and that it is therefore possible to say
whether these things are suited to them. These would then be
constitutive of the good life (A. Brown, 1986: 135). He offers one
such set of basic human goods as a starter:

1 The means of subsistence; adequate food, clothing, shelter
   and so on.
2 Pleasure. . . . Human beings do indeed value pleasure for
   its own sake, so that it can be described as an irreducible
   aspect of the truly good life.
3 Work, rest and play; these constitute the basic activities that
   human beings must engage in if their lives are to be well-
   balanced, if they are to develop as human beings.
4 Social relationships: these constitute the proper social context for the pursuit of the basic good activities, and reflect
   the fact that we have social, and not just private, needs. (A.
   Brown, 1986: 159)

There will of course be endless debates about what constitutes,
say, a good form of work or play. Further, each class of good is
elastic. In other words, we can have too much or too little of each.
Nevertheless, each of the basic goods must be present to some extent
for life to be as good as it can be:

The idea is that the proper enjoyment of each class of good
leads to self-development, flourishing or the good life. But

these . . . are not some further good or end to which the basic
goods are merely means. The good life is but the name we give
to a life which successfully combines the basic goods.
(A. Brown, 1986: 160)

For goods to be reconciled and ordered it is necessary to engage in
a process of practical reasoning and it is not possible to use simple
rules or procedures such as those associated with Rawls's principles
of justice or that of utility. However, having established that if a life
is to be as good as it can be, i.e. it must include all the basic goods, it
is possible to discover the proper extent of engagement in each basic
good through trial and error. Individuals can of course look beyond
their immediate experience for guidance. Science and commonsense
understandings may provide some indication of proportion. As the
pursuit of the goods will usually involve the cooperation of others,
such activity has to be coordinated. 'The need to live in a society
which has definite social structures will impose a system on the pursuit of the good – it will dictate norms of family life, economic activity, creative pursuits and so on' (A. Brown, 1986: 161). Knowing
that good will be fostered best in certain types of social structure, it is
logical to accept the rules and restrictions generated by that structure
which relate to the basic goods.

Educators and well-being

If we now consider what might be the role of educators in relation to
this way of proceeding, and here we are heavily dependent on the
work of White (1982), then it is apparent that their tasks will be
three-fold. First, individuals have to understand in general terms
what their well-being consists in. They have to see themselves as animals with an array of desires, 'and to appreciate the way in which
these desires may take different forms owing to cultural influences
and new desires of all kinds be built out of them' (White, 1982: 58).
This process is both expansionary (it opens up doors) and restrictive
(i.e. choices have to be made).

Secondly, the educational task must include the development of
competencies in relation to the attainment of such basic human
goods. This involves the development of skills in relationships, in
obtaining the means of subsistence, in work and so on.

Thirdly, and crucially, the possession of general understandings
and skills is not enough – educators also have a fundamental role in
shaping dispositions. In other words, people need to gain various
dispositions or virtues which enable them to fit all this together into a
coherent whole.

To proceed it is necessary to address questions surrounding the relationship of the individual to the collectivity: the extent to which education is for the good of the individual or the collectivity. There is a tension between education as an activity which seeks to offer benefits to individuals and education which is designed primarily to meet 'society's needs'. When understood in terms of the longstanding problem of the relationship of person-centred to moral aims in education, then a number of ways of attempting to resolve such tensions are apparent (White, 1982: 68–92). The first is simply to assert that the individual's good is identical with the good of others. In a situation of scarce resources and limited opportunities this argument is difficult to sustain. At some point individuals pursuing their own interests must clash in such a way as to make the term 'common good' meaningless.

A second course is to assume that an individual's good should be of central importance to her/him within a framework of minimum moral duties. It is in the individual's self interest, as in everybody elses', for there to be generally accepted moral rules providing a framework within which people can serve their own ends. This sounds like the morality of the market, of the pursuit of profit within a minimal framework of rules. As might be expected, this course also leaves a range of questions unanswered – how extensive are the moral obligations involved? To what extent should the individual promote the well-being of others? 'The choices for the minimal moralist seem to be irrational rule-worship on the one hand or free-riding on the other' (White, 1982: 84).

The third possibility is universalistic – individuals should work self-sacrificingly for the good of humanity. Not only is this a denial of the worth of the individual and the self, it would also appear to fly in the face of what we know of human nature. To put forward as a morality something which, even if it were admirable, would be an impossible ideal, is likely to do more harm than good. 'It encourages the treatment of moral principles not as guides to action but as a fantasy which accompanies actions with which it is quite incompatible (Mackie, 1977: 131–2).

A fourth possibility is to argue that individuals should work for the good of small communities, which, being small, help them to realize their own well-being. These small communities are, in turn, nested within larger communities, so linking individuals to humankind as a whole. This argument faces similar problems as the first, but at least has the appeal of making moral obligations concrete, that is to say operating around people in face-to-face situations. However, there are major problems here concerning the nature of the relationship between the localized community and the larger one about the extent of boundaries.

White, having reviewed the four options, proceeds to argue that a solution is possible via the idea of autonomy and an enlarged understanding of well-being (1982: 92–103). Education, he argues, should aim at individuals autonomously pursuing their own well-being. To be autonomous requires that people have a developed self, to which their actions can be ascribed. 'In turn this requires a consciousness of oneself as a being who acts for reasons, whose behaviour can be explained by reference to one's own goals and purposes' (Lindley, 1986: 6). A second dimension of autonomy requires freedom from external constraints. That is to say, an autonomous person is someone who is not manipulated by others. Such a person is able to act in pursuit of self-chosen goals. However, autonomy on its own is not enough to get around the problems of reconciling person-centred and moral aims. We might be left with a 'solution' looking uncomfortably like one of those already rejected.

One way forward is to introduce the idea of responsibilities as, for example, the Grubb Institute has done when defining that state of being known as 'adulthood':

> To be an adult is to remain in touch with your capacities and responsibilities whatever the relation between the context and oneself. (quoted in YMCA, 1986: 3)

The definition is reminiscent of some of the conceptions of social education discussed in the last chapter and could be attractive to those seeking some purpose in youth work. Its particular virtue is the emphasis upon 'connectedness', which presumably means something more than simply knowing one's limits and duties. It also involves relating the different attitudes and motives that a person may hold and becoming conscious of their contradictions. Aside from questions as to whether the word 'adult' with all its other meanings is a helpful way of labelling this state, a major problem facing this definition is that it only has a flimsy theory of the good when compared with well-being. For example, it says little directly about the nature of the responsibilities. Essentially what is said is that to be in touch is to be good.

White skates around some of these problems by enlarging what people may understand of their own 'well-being'. The well-being that educators should help individuals to pursue involves leading a life of moral virtue. In this life, the individual's own needs should not automatically be given preferential treatment but be weighed in relation to the needs of others (1982: 98). The process by which this

weighing takes place returns us to the concerns of the opening section of the chapter. There it was argued that the purpose of the political community should be the pursuit of the good. This good is the
good of the individual members of the community. The good life is
one which involves all the basic goods to the proper extent. Thus the
good society is one which promotes such lives, at least as a prime
objective (A. Brown, 1986: 166–7) and good people are those who
seek the basic goods to the proper extent in both their own, and
generally in others', lives.

Individuals cannot make decisions about what constitutes well-
being in this enlarged sense without reference to others. The scale
and nature of such cooperation would appear to take us beyond the
sort of minimalist position already dismissed. In other words, the
full development of any individual requires the presence of sophisticated and convivial social structures. This very reliance on social
relations should lead people 'to reject any social system which
systematically denies anyone access to any basic goods if an
improvement is possible – even where that improvement will
impose costs in terms of other goods to some' (A. Brown, 1986: 169).

For individuals to understand and care that their own well-being
consists in weighing their own needs and interests with those of
others, they also require a social and political system which allows
such individual decisions to be made and carried out and which
ensures access to basic goods. Manifestly, liberal or bourgeois democratic societies have failed to realize the development, maintenance
and exercise of autonomy (Lindley, 1986: 187). Capitalism, whether
private or state, has been unable to deliver the proper distribution of
basic human goods. As a result, the task of educators is not merely to
help people to develop their own understanding of what exists and
what is good, they must also work with people so that they may
answer the question 'what is to be done?' Such political or citizenship
education is not simply about knowledge, it also has to do with attitudes and feelings, and with the acquisition of appropriate skills (M.
Smith, 1987: 3–8). Knowing what to do is not enough, people
must also have the disposition and capacity to act, so that they may
challenge and attempt to transform the political, social and economic forces which deny them well-being. They must be educated to
display civic courage:

> one should think and act as if one were in a real democracy.
> The fundamental bravery of this way of life is not military
> heroism but civic courage. Whoever says no to the dominant
> prejudices and to the oppressing power, and when necessary
> (and it is often necessary) to public opinion, and practises this

throughout his life and in his life-conduct has the virtue of civic courage. (Heller, 1976: 202)

Developing civic courage and the other knowledge, attitudes and skills necessary to understand and act upon the institutions and processes which significantly affect well-being is a daunting task and places a number of duties upon the educator as Giroux has indicated (1983: 202–3). First, the active nature of people's participation in the learning process must be stressed. Learning relationships have to be structured to facilitate dialogue and critical engagement (see Chapter 7). Secondly, people must be taught to think critically. They need to be able to engage in questioning, problem-posing and theory-making which connects with the situations they find themselves in. Thirdly, 'the development of a critical mode of reasoning must be used to enable students to appropriate their own histories, i.e. to delve into their own biographies and systems of meaning' (Giroux, 1983: 202–3). A critical education will provide the conditions for people to address their own culture, to own their experiences and thinking, and hence to speak with their own voices. Fourthly, people must also learn what is good, they must learn what values are central to human life and well-being and how such values are transmitted and tortured in the interests of the powerful. Finally, people must learn about the structural and ideological forces which influence and restrict their lives:

> The order of priorities, the scale of values in our everyday life is largely taken over ready-made, it is calibrated in accordance with position in society, and little on it is movable. There is little opportunity to 'cultivate' our abilities beyond, at best, very narrow confines. (Heller, 1984: 15)

Part of the educator's task is to enable opportunities, however limited, to help people to gain the necessary knowledge, skills and attitudes in order that they may push back the boundaries within which they may act for the good.

We can now see the wholeness of the educational enterprise. While the focus here may be on the political, 'the human meaning of public issues must be revealed by relating them to personal troubles – and to the problems of the individual life' (Mills, 1970: 248). The questions 'what exists, what is good and what is to be done?' relate as much to the individual self as to the context in which it exists. If individuals are to pursue their own well-being autonomously, and if there is to be an 'association, in which the free development of each is the condition for the free development of all'

(Marx and Engels, 1888: 76), then educators must help people to achieve a state of active and critical connectedness or *nexus* both within and beyond their selves in order that the proper balance of basic goods may be achieved.

Before leaving this discussion it is necessary to reflect upon the relevance here of the criticisms made of social education in the last chapter. First, it should be noted that the approach adopted, by enlarging the notion of well-being and by recognizing the fundamental importance of social relations and structures, has been able to reconcile person-centredness with broader political and moral aims. Secondly, while the dangers of paternalism and the use of contested notions such as adolescence remain, they are strongly counter-balanced by an insistence that education should aim at individuals autonomously pursuing their own well-being. Enabling people to act in pursuit of self-chosen goals requires the educator to operate so that young people may take responsibility for their learning. Thirdly, there must be some question as to the ethnocentricity of this model, just as there was in the discussion of social education. At one level autonomy is a liberal notion, yet great value has also been placed upon it within classical Marxism. However, it is not a universal feature of all cultures. Thus, the central question is whether it is objectively valid, whether people ought to be brought up to be autonomous (White, 1982: 128). Such a state requires a developed sense of the self and a will of one's own, that people should be free to choose and take responsibility for their own actions. In order to ameliorate, but not dispose of, the charge of cultural aggression, specific attention must be paid to the nature of the self. This sense of self may be Hindu, Shinto, Confucian, whatever. In other words, people may *choose* to be dependent on selected others. Hence, the thinking advanced here may be universally applicable. That is to say it may be acceptable to particular elements within broad cultures. However, many would dispute the notion of autonomy and the implications it may have for life.

Youth workers as educators

Thus far we have been able to progress without actually saying what education is and why it should be the focus of identity for youth workers. To 'educate' was originally to rear or bring up children or animals, its root apparently lying in *educere*, to lead forth (Williams, 1976: 95). In this way education was age-specific, essentially applying to children. The content was to be found in 'the culture which each generation purposely gives to those who are to be its successors, in order to qualify them for at least keeping up, and if possible for raising, the level of improvement which has been attained' (Mill, 1867). However, such an inter-generational perspective is inadequate as learning continues through life. While people may be described as educated, that is not a fixed state, they can never know or be able to do everything. In addition, education either can be self-directed or facilitated by others. But, such a conclusion should not be allowed to blur 'the vital distinction between a person's upbringing, which for him cannot be voluntary, and his adult learning activities, whether cultural or occupational, which should be voluntary' (White, 1982: 132).

It is also apparent that education is intentional, i.e. people *seek* to improve themselves or *try* to help others learn. As part of the process people have to manage the external conditions that facilitate the internal change called learning (Brookfield, 1986: 46). In other words, there has to be some plan for learning. From this we have an understanding of education as a process which is to some extent planned and aimed at facilitating learning. However, such is the breadth of this understanding, that a number of other forms of interventions can also come under its aegis. It may be that the phenomenon is so complex as to be beyond adequate definition, but at this stage things do not look so hopeless. It is possible to approach a broad definition. We have already seen that education is incorrigibly normative and idealistic and it is this that Jarvis picks on to define education as 'any planned series of incidents, having a humanistic basis, directed towards the participants learning and understanding' (1983a: 5, 1983b: 26). In focusing upon a humanistic basis, let us return to Dewey:

> Knowledge is humanistic in quality not because it is *about* human products in the past, but because of what it *does* in liberating human intelligence and human sympathy. Any subject matter which accomplishes this result is humane, and any subject matter which does not accomplish it is not even educational. (Dewey, 1916: 230).

Humanism 'means at bottom being imbued with an intelligent sense of human interests' (Dewey, 1916: 288), and while its invocation may separate education from indoctrination, it does not set it aside from, say, therapy. At one level this is because therapy inevitably involves education, but further differentiation is possible as soon as we examine the balance of theories appealed to and practices used. These are reflected, to some extent, in the contrast between the social and personal development and welfaring traditions of youth work (see Chapter 3); in the contrast of developmental psychology with psychoanalytical theory and abnormal psychology; in a concern with 'normal' people rather than those 'in trouble'; and in different frameworks for contact (Hudson, 1984: 48–9).

The question now arises, why should youth workers appeal to educational ideas and practices as the central point of orientation in their occupational identity? Given scarce resources, the key consideration is the extent to which the adoption of an educational as against any other youth work identity promotes lives in which all the basic goods are involved to the proper extent. This is a deeply political question and at this point we have to enter the messy world of existing institutions, traditions and practices. Historically two themes have dominated the discussion of purpose in youth work: education and amusement. In the case of the latter, the simple provision of opportunities for social relationships or for play does nothing directly to enable people to gain the necessary knowledge, skills and attitudes in order that they may make use of such openings. Secondly, it allows moral and political calculations as to what is proper or good and how individuals weigh their own and others' interests to go by the board. At this simple level the case for education is clear. Furthermore, it will be argued that the nature and shape of many youth work institutions and traditions are peculiarly suited to particular educational tasks. If they did not exist, something very much like them would have to be invented.

Against this we must consider the claims of other forms of intervention: the therapeutic, the provision of material goods, the creation of opportunities for vocational skilling and so on. Two questions are central here: what does youth work possess which makes it especially disposed to particular forms of intervention, and what can or do other agencies offer? In the case of the former, the weight of history lies heavily in education's favour; in the latter, as we saw in Chapter 4, powerful institutions already exist with the potential, if not the disposition and direction, to promote lives in which all the basic goods are involved to the proper extent.

Youth workers need to commit themselves fully to making a choice. Those not solidly locked into a particular youth work tradition are likely to lack a coherent occupational identity. Not having that deep sense of place and purpose not only leaves them vulnerable to fads and fashions, but it is also personally debilitating and unsettling. They lack a home in the world and, as such, have difficulties 'making sense' (Heller, 1983: 65). For their work to proceed they will have to name their essence.

Educators in the community

If youth workers accept they are educators and that they should aim
to enable individuals to pursue their own well-being autonomously,
then it is necessary to define what their distinctive contribution is.
Educators in other institutions have expanded their work with
young people and have adopted many of the concerns, methods and
rationales associated with youth work. While schools, for example,
may experience difficulties in providing appropriate programmes to
enable social and personal development, their scope and scale dwarf
those of youth work. Within what has been advanced here there is a
clear rationale for their interventions with young people in this
respect. Given that significant intellectual, physiological and social
developments are associated with youth, there should be a desire to
enable young people to understand what their well-being consists of
in relation to these. At the same time these developments strengthen
the conditions that allow individuals to pursue their own well-being
autonomously. Should then these concerns be the central focus for
youth workers? The very expansion of other agencies into this arena
and their relative success and potential suggests that youth workers
must offer something very special in this respect if they are to remain
relevant in welfare. One such candidate could be their potential as
educators in the community.

Schooling rarely engages in a sustained way with networks
beyond those immediately presented within its walls. Further, as
Rogers and Groombridge have argued about adults: 'most . . .
learning goes on outside the classroom and always will. It is such a
mundane and familiar activity that it is easy to overlook how
deliberately and constantly many millions of adults are seeking to
learn something new' (1976: 58). Where educators do seek to connect, where they work 'in the community', they are often set apart
from teachers. At one level, making such a distinction between
school and community is nonsensical. The school is part of the local
social systems that many would see as constituting the community.
In this sense, educators are as much in the community when teaching
third years French, as when engaged in a heated discussion about
modern art in the Over-60s Club. However, when approached symbolically a rather different picture emerges, a picture which places a
special emphasis on people's experience and perceptions, and the
way in which they construct and use boundaries in order to give substance to their values and identities (Cohen, 1985). Wallman has
used the device of a person's 'locus of identity' to good effect in this

respect (1984: 214). To call someone an educator in the community is to say that their identity as an educator is sustained in significant ways by the structures and forms which they associate with that entity. These structures may be provided by religious bodies, family gatherings, hobbyists' societies, tenants associations, street-corner groups, neighbourly networks, and a myriad of other everyday situations. In some, education will be the central focus, in others just one consideration among many. Often the role of the educator in these situations is to enable individuals and groups to identify, plan, resource, carry out and evaluate their own learning projects. The educator's expertise is in the process of education, rather than in the specific topic for ultimate study.

Youth workers with a remit to work as educators in the community may offer their educational process skills in much the same way. The learning projects that young people identify may well differ from those of older age groups, given the particular social, physical and emotional experiences associated with youth. Indeed, it is easy to predict what some of the main themes will be. However, the central point about this relationship is that the educator does not seek to bring a particular curriculum to young people, other than that associated with the process of learning and with the values that it expresses and implies.

Alternatively, youth workers may actively seek the adoption of a particular curriculum, such as in the various programmes associated with health education. Here the desire might be to raise awareness and competence in relation to particular areas such as childcare, solvent abuse and AIDs. However, entry and the resulting programme still have to be negotiated and this entails a different relationship between practitioners and young people than that which usually exists within schools or, indeed, within much youth work. It is more akin to the relationship between community workers and neighbourhood groups. In the school or youth club, practitioners usually see themselves as being responsible for what happens. Youth workers manage buildings, initiate groups, organize programmes, arrange equipment and take the blame when things go wrong. Community workers may do all or some of these things, but the balance is different, and this may arise from their more generalized respect for the integrity and responsibilities of the groups they work alongside.

All this implies a vital shift in the rationale for working with young people, one which recognizes a movement from the compulsory sphere of upbringing towards the voluntary concerns of adult learning activities. The new rationale for working with young people would be first because they are 'there'. In other words, part of the reason for working with youth is that 'youth' appears to have meaning in the lives of a particular group of people. Young people seek out each other's company, want to do things together, seem to feel that there are particular problems about being 'young'. The second reason for wanting to work with this group is that it would appear that at this particular moment people, for the first time, are attempting to step outside themselves in order to make sense of the world. While it is clear that change is possible throughout life, the apparent fact that young people are beginning to think in a different way should signal a change in the sort of work that can be done and the relationship of the educator to them.

The pedagogic assumptions underlying these approaches are clearly in line with what has been said about purpose in this chapter: the processes would appear to be capable of helping individuals to pursue their own well-being autonomously; however, content would have to be judged on the particular individual(s). Certainly, there is a strong case for this form of intervention with young people and one to which youth workers could make a significant contribution. But is this contribution distinctive? A very similar argument is advanced by community schoolers (see Allen *et al.*, 1987) and it is difficult to escape the conclusion that it is school structures and processes which must be reorientated. Thus, while this activity is worthwhile and youth workers may have a role, there remains a question as to whether it should be their primary focus.

Enlarging understandings of well-being

To get any further we must return to our initial discussion of education and ascertain what elements are handled inadequately, and what cannot be effectively and wholly pursued within central institutions such as the school and household. Immediately it is apparent that there is a lack of attention to helping young people to understand well-being in the extended sense, to develop civic courage and to enable them to think and act politically. Further, households are unable to fully handle these matters themselves. Individuals join other groupings such as religious bodies, cultural organizations and political parties so as to work at practical, political and moral questions, to celebrate and maintain their beliefs and to influence others. In addition, schooling has failed to enable people to act collectively in the world and to learn from it.

Entwistle (1971) has provided one of the best known explorations of the school as an institution which can be used to develop young people's political knowledge and skills. He examines some of the areas, such as school societies and councils, where students can become involved in decision making processes that affect the institution. The most obvious criticism of such work is that pupils are only 'playing at politics' and are not engaged in real politics at all, 'for real politics is about power upon which real and important differences of outcome may depend' (Wringe, 1984: 102). This point is underlined by Entwistle himself, when he says that 'the government of most schools still approximates to that of the totalitarian state rather than to a democratic model' (1971: 35). In effect, schools councils and the like do not provide education in participant democracy at all, but education in leadership for the few and political passivity for the majority.

Other approaches do seek to put young people into direct contact with the political systems beyond the school. Here the idea may be to encourage young people in their efforts to find expression for their own views or those of the community of which they are a part. This may result in active campaigning around issues as diverse as nuclear disarmament or the lack of bus shelters. A major problem occurs here in that such groupings of young people will not be organizationally separate from the school. Not only does this mean that actions of the group will directly reflect upon the school and their freedom be limited, but it also severely hampers the potential for learning as people are not in a position to take responsibility for their actions. In other words, young people are denied the opportunity to form and guide what Entwistle calls 'micro-institutions'. Such institutions are an integral part of his advocacy of 'associational democracy':

> This conception is based on the assumption that it is those micro-institutions (economic, cultural, educational, religious, philanthropic, recreational) encountered by people in their daily lives which offer them the reality of participating in the management of affairs which touch them closely in relation to their work, their play, their domestic affairs, as well as in their dispositions to be altruistic or charitable in relation to their fellow men. . . . Nor is associational democracy merely the politics of the parish pump. Voluntary associations are the channels through which, for most of us, engagement with politics at the macro-level is possible. (Entwistle, 1981: 245)

A lack of such intermediate institutions or mediating structures, 'not only leaves the individual vulnerable in times of crisis – as for example, when in need of social care – but threatens the political order by depriving it of the moral foundations on which it rests' (Bulmer, 1987: 68). They provide a focus for social, political and religious activity and a point of attachment.

It is exactly these sorts of institutions which youth work provides. The groups that practitioners work with and within frequently have an organizational status independent of the State. Thus, while a proportion of workers may be state-employed and bound by specific policies, the groups which they assist are not. They are in a position to make choices and face consequences. Their 'associational' or voluntary status involve structures that are open to a certain amount of direct participation by the membership or local community, and that engage with political institutions at the macro level. Some groupings can be considered as organized forms of mutual aid, 'through which enthusiasts combine together to produce goods and services for their own enjoyment' (Bishop and Hoggett, 1986: 4). In this we have a site for a participant political or citizenship education that is a good deal more convivial than that afforded by the school. Indeed, it is necessary that such institutions have an identity quite separate from the school as we know it, for it is essential that they are owned by their members. However, while recognizing that the school is structurally unable to provide the context for certain forms of work, learning from those forms must find its way back into the school if charges of marginalization are to be avoided.

Furthermore, we also have to recognize that the bulk of those engaged in youth work are in fact not paid and are often part of the community from which the membership of their groups are drawn. This contrasts strongly with professionalized forms where practitioners and sponsors tend to make little reference to, and have little or no previous connection with, the social systems and cultures with which they have to work. The level of shared assumption, of common experience and of similar prospects may be higher than that within professionalized interventions. It may also be that such workers have not been able to step outside their experiences, to reflect upon the reasons for their practice and the things that they might aim for. However, this problem is surmountable by bringing educators imbued with a critical perspective into an engagement with these organic youth work forms. There is then the chance to provide a context in which people can interrogate their own culture and develop a new understanding of it.

In addition to the particular qualities of structures and personnel, certain traditions of practice connect very strongly with the desire to enlarge people's appreciation of what their own well-being might consist of. Here, we can return to the concerns of Chapter 3 and, in particular, the qualities that many workers within the social and leisure traditions seek to promote.

Here lies the special contribution that workers in youth organizations can make. They may not be able to lay exclusive claims on the methods, concerns and purposes they utilize, but their personal qualities, the institutions in which they operate, and the nature of certain traditions of practice hold the key to youth workers' relevance as educators. They can make a special contribution to the development of people's understanding of, commitment to and competencies in the processes that allow individuals to act together to promote well-being or human flourishing. To say this is not only to argue for a basic shift towards educative practice, but also to assert that the primary focus in youth work should move away from a near exclusive concern with the self and immediate others. It is also to view those who argue that youth work should be directed at groups of young people with particular 'deficits' with great suspicion. Here, youth work is conceived as a universal phenomenon. Its practitioners should be working to enlarge people's understanding of their own well-being so that they weigh their own needs and interests with those of others, to help people to display civic courage, and to enable people to gain for themselves the knowledge, attitudes and skills necessary to think and act politically.

With the emphasis being so firmly placed upon education, it does raise questions as to the continuing appropriateness of the designation 'youth work'. It is work with youth, but of a particular kind. Often, for other external reasons, a number of LEAs have already given workers such titles as 'Community Educators (Youth)'. Alternatively, we might define workers by the methods they use, e.g. informal education (see Chapter 7), or the forms they work with, e.g. the everyday. Having already sounded the death knell for the Youth Service, we could extend the peel to the appellation 'youth work'. Yet that would be premature; such titles are not wholly matters of logic. They are expressive of certain traditions of thinking and acting. The title may change as those change and, for the moment, there would appear to be a strong allegiance to 'youth work', particularly within the central, popular traditions of the work. For this reason we may as well stay with youth work, but do so knowing that as practitioners develop their understandings and identity, they may wish to construct a new vocabulary and rename themselves.

Chapter 7

Informal Education

Having dismissed social education as a description of method and made some assertions concerning purpose in youth work, it is necessary to reassess and rehabilitate the notion of informal education. Unfortunately, within youth work, informal education has become entwined with that of social education. For example, the Albemarle Report asserted that the Youth Service provides 'for the continued social and informal education of young people in terms most likely to bring them to maturity, those of responsible personal choice' (HMSO, 1960: 103). Goetschius and Tash argued for the use of 'the tools and techniques of informal education. The method might best be described as social education' (1967: 134). This apparent absorption of the informal within the sphere of social education helps explain why the concept has rarely appeared in contemporary debates and discussions within youth work. Similarly, the growth of interest within schooling in social education and in schemes such as Active Tutorial Work, combined with a general shift towards extra-mural leisure provision has contributed to the lack of critical attention to the informal within that sector. The story is little different in community work, where 'the lacunae about informal educational goals and methods . . . were the most important consequences of the withdrawal of educationalists from community work in the 1970s' (Thomas, 1983: 32).

While the usage of 'informal' may often appear confused, its very familiarity and association with ideas which articulate the processes under consideration still make it an attractive label for method. For example, 'informal' is commonly used to indicate that something is not of an official or stiffly conventional nature; is appropriate to everyday life or use (such as informal clothes); or is characterized by the idiom and vocabulary appropriate to everyday conversational language, rather than formal written language (Collins English Dictionary, 1979). These are very suggestive meanings and are worth pursuing.

Informal education and its alternatives

Informal education is often used to describe the learning activities of everyday life. These are then contrasted with those that occur within the 'formality' of the school or college. To this may be added further categories such as the non-formal:

Formal education: the hierarchically structured, chronologically graded 'education system', running from primary school through the university and including, in addition to general academic studies, a variety of specialized programmes and institutions for full-time technical and professional training.

Informal education: the truly lifelong process whereby every individual acquires attitudes, values, skills and knowledge from daily experience and the educative influences and resources in his or her environment – from family and neighbours, from work and play, from the market place, the library and the mass media.

Non-formal education: any organized educational activity outside the established formal system – whether operating separately or as an important feature of some broader activity – that is intended to serve identifiable learning clienteles and learning objectives. (Coombs, 1973, quoted in Fordham *et al.*, 1979: 210–11)

There are major problems involved in categorizations such as these. These can be demonstrated through a consideration of Jensen *et al.*'s (1964) well-known distinction between 'natural societal settings' and 'formal instructional settings': the former being described as the everyday world of individual experience – in the family, at work, at play – where learning is often regarded as incidental; and the latter settings where an 'educational agent' takes on responsibility for planning and managing instruction so that the learner achieves some previously specified object. Presumably this covers both the non-formal and formal categories of Coombs *et al.* (1973).

First, on a narrow definition, 'educational agents' could be considered to be people only in the employ or under the jurisdiction of recognized educational institutions who have as their prime task enabling people to learn. This would seem unnecessarily restrictive. A more helpful course would be to consider anybody who consciously helps another person to learn as an educational agent, whether that help is given directly or takes the form of deliberately creating an appropriate environment to facilitate learning.

Secondly, there are often occasions when formal instructional settings are created within those environments labelled as natural societal settings. Thus, short courses in management might take place within a community association, individuals may arrange sessions with an expert in their chosen interest or hobby, and the study of theology by house groups may occur in a religious organization. This poses particular problems for the distinction made between informal and non-formal education by Coombs *et al*. (1973). The 'life-long processes' of informal education can actually involve organized educational activity with learning objectives.

Finally, while there may seem to be a commonsense difference in settings, the examples given – the workplace, home and leisure – are no more or less 'natural' than a school or college. Work organizations, social clubs, sports centres and families are constructed with a purpose. In this they are no different to 'formal instructional settings'. However, what could be different are the explicit and implicit purposes to which they are put.

With similar processes occurring within two, or possibly all three of Coombs *et al*.'s (1973) categories, the bases of these divisions looks suspect. The introduction of the notion of non-formal education simply confuses the situation. Further divisions via the nature of the setting add little on their own. To progress it is necessary to examine the characteristics of the learning process and the way in which they interact with objectives and the setting or institution in which the activity is placed. In this way we can begin to make sense of the attraction of the notion of informal education.

What is informal education?

As we have seen, the nature of the setting is one of the basic elements used when describing informal education. It is the first of seven elements I wish to advance as characterizing informal education. We must begin by noting that informal education can happen within a wide variety of settings, many of which are used by others at the same time for completely different purposes. Examples of these would be clubs and pubs. Further, if we consider process, rather than simply institutional sponsorship or a normative idea of setting, then it becomes apparent that informal education may also occur within schools and colleges. Perhaps the most obvious examples would be the forms of learning associated with free-time or after-school clubs and activities and timetabled activities that students can choose to attend or not.

Secondly, a central consideration has been the apparently incidental manner in which learning may occur in informal or 'natural societal' situations. As Brookfield notes, we should not fall into the trap of equating incidental with accidental:

> Although learning occurring outside schools, colleges and universities may be unplanned and accidental, there must be much that is purposeful and deliberate . . . the circumstances occasioning learning may often be outside the individual's control; for example an enforced job change, childbirth, conscription. However, the individual who decides that the acquisition of certain skills and knowledge is essential to managing such crises and changes successfully is behaving in a highly purposeful manner. (Brookfield, 1983: 12–13)

In addition, it should be remembered that much of what happens within formal instructional settings is unplanned and has unintended outcomes, even though the task focus is on learning and that this involves planning curricula, choosing methods and creating an appropriately ordered milieu.

The question of curricula, or rather of learning objectives, is a crucial one. Lawson has written of the looseness of the concept of 'learning situation'. He regards this as being so general that it is of little use as a guide to educational practice:

> If all learning, in any circumstances, is regarded as education it is impossible to order priorities and meaningless to talk of educational methods and standards because 'learning situations' in the unqualified sense develop regardless of priorities, methods or standards; they simply happen. (Lawson, 1974: 88)

On this view, that which is acquired in casual encounters or in many youth work, social work or community work settings does not fulfil an essential educational criterion, in that learning objectives may not be shared by both parties. While, undoubtedly, there is a high degree of looseness about 'learning situation', it is dangerous to define the learning process over-restrictedly. Much rests on what is meant by 'objectives' and by 'shared'. For example, there has to be some question as to the degree to which objectives are actually known and agreed to both 'teacher' and 'learner' in so-called formal instructional settings. Are pupils in primary schools fully aware of the curriculum, for example? While there may be an agreed broad purpose, objectives may not be shared and agreed. Hence the equating of deliberation and intention in learning with the pursuit of previously specified learning objectives requires special attention.

Central to this consideration is the specificity of objectives and the point at which they are agreed. The process of learning inevitably involves the constant reformulation of objectives as learners develop their understanding. New questions become apparent, other avenues of thought open up. Thus, while learners may be operating within a broadly agreed area, their activities may well take them in unpredictable directions. Perhaps the important distinction is that between aims and objectives. Aims could be conceived of as the ultimate goal, where objectives are the steps by which aims are achieved. To be effective, such objectives will be specific, measurable and have some indication of when they are to be achieved. In this sense the broad direction is given by the aim and specifics by the objective. Thus only a narrow range of endeavours, often linked to examination, could really be said to be characterized by having previously specified objectives in this sense. Dewey (1933), in discussing the role of reflection in learning, presents the activity as purposeful, although the goals may not be clear at the time either to the educator or to the learner. Learners know that they need to sort something out – to put information and feelings in order. Hence learning is deliberate and purposeful in that the people concerned are seeking to acquire some knowledge, skills and/or attitudes. However, the purpose and intent may not always be marked by closely specified goals (Brookfield, 1983: 15).

A third characteristic concerns time structuring. The initial conclusion might be that informal education does not follow timetables, and is not linked to the forms of time organizing associated with schooling and higher education. While there may not be terms, periods, breaks and academic years, forms of time structuring will be present, usually influenced by the institution or setting where the work takes place. For example, pubs and clubs have opening times, there are such things as public holidays, and everyday living inevitably follows certain patterns. Further, many of the settings that informal education could be said to take place within, are linked with academic timetables. These might include school-based youth provision and youth work that is located within local education authorities. Many of those young people engaged in informal learning will also be at school and, for the most part, will therefore only be available for youth work at those times when the school is not operating.

A further question that arises in relation to time is the extent to which interventions have a future and a past. Not possessing some of the formalized conventions concerning attendance, and not necessarily having a contract for work over time, informal education can take the form of discrete interventions. There can be a 'one-off' quality to some of the work. None the less, the work does not occur in a vacuum and it is often the case that 'contracts' are made that involve considerable time spans. Thus, such forms of learning do not lack time structuring, but the structuring is highly variable and can alter according to the particular learning project, the nature of the group and the impact of any number of other, external elements such as 'closing time'.

Fourthly, people participate in informal education by choice. They engage in learning as a result of their own volition. This element has been asserted because it connects with the fluidity of informal education practice and the disposition necessary for the fulfilment of other characteristics. Thus, while attendance at school may be compulsory, there will be times when participation in certain activities is not required, and when informal educational activities may take place. As involvement is voluntary, there is an assumption that educators do not have to spend large amounts of time on the sorts of control questions that so occupy school teachers. However, important control questions are present. A central problem in this respect is how to control the intrusion of the 'external world' into the learning process, be it in the form of music, drunks or toddlers. Another problem concerns how to keep people 'on the point' if the situation is 'informal'. In addition, voluntary participation does imply a degree of motivation but, crucially, it also means that participation can often be withdrawn at a moment's notice.

Fifthly, informal education is informed by considerable responsiveness between educator and learner and between learner and learner. In other words, it involves a high degree of dialogue. As Moore has argued, this can be determined by the content or subject matter which is explored, by the educational philosophy of the educator, by the personalities of educator and learner and by environmental factors, most important of which is the medium of communication (1983: 157). Undoubtedly the most common medium within informal education is the spoken word, which clearly makes for responsiveness. The notion of dialogue also implies a particular kind of relationship between educator and learner and between learners, one which is based upon mutual respect. All this is discussed at some length later in the chapter.

Sixthly, informal education is distinguished by the use of familiar cultural forms and social systems. Rather than create an institution largely separated from, or beyond the day-to-day context in which people operate, informal educators will attempt to work within or alongside forms and structures familiar to, and owned by, participants. This requires an active appreciation of local social systems and the culture of those engaged. The danger here, of course, is of making a false separation between, say, 'the school' and 'the community'. On almost all counts, the school is pre-eminently part of the community; however, the staff may not *feel* themselves to be. This subjective dimension can be encapsulated in the phrase 'locus of identity' (Wallman, 1984: 214). Thus, informal educators' identities as educators are linked with a commitment to making exchanges with the social systems and culture through which learners operate. That identity tends to be less with their immediate institution, and rather more with the learning processes that can be generated within everyday life. Indeed one way of thinking about informal education is as the informed use of the everyday in order to enable learning. It may be that informal educators identify with the values and view of the world expressed by members of the particular local system, but this need not be the case. However, the essential point is that informal educators adopt or work with cultural forms familiar to those involved. In doing so they may seek to confront them in some way.

Finally, for many practitioners, informal education is synonymous with a pattern of learning that might be described as experiential, 'education that occurs as a result of direct participation in the events of life' (Houle, 1980: 221). Such a pattern starts with concrete experience, with people doing things. Then, so the model goes, there is a period of reflection and theory-making which leads again to the testing out of new understandings and more concrete experiences (Kolb, 1976). This pattern is contrasted with that which is supposed to reside in formal educational institutions – a process of information assimilation. Here, the process begins with the educator transmitting information through some symbolic medium such as a lecture. The learner then receives information, assimilates and organizes it, uses the general principle gained to infer a particular application, and then takes action (Coleman, 1976: 50). Yet, even a cursory examination of practice soon reveals that both patterns of learning are in use within informal education approaches. There will be times when educators or learners may need to communicate ideas and information in a comprehensive and organized form and will therefore need to utilize the information assimilation pattern. At other moments it will be necessary to begin with an experience and to develop a generalized understanding from it.

The focus upon starting points and the debates between those advocating experiential or information assimilation methods tends to divert attention from the process that follows. As Dewey noted in the context of the debate between so-called traditional and progressive education, there is the inherent danger that principles are formed by reaction, 'instead of by a comprehensive, constructive survey of actual needs, problems and possibilities' (1938: 6). By becoming wrapped up in the starting point, it often seems that the simple provision of information or experience is enough. The rest of the process is largely ignored and, hence, any understanding of the educative role is somewhat limited. If the information or experience is not interrogated, reflected upon and some theory developed, then there appears to be little educative point to the exercise. A major problem is that within the sort of settings we are considering here, even where there is some appreciation of the need for attention to reflection and theory-making, not enough time may be given over to such activity. This may be a result of inadequate pedagogic skills, though more often it is an outcome of the fact that in the heat of a particular activity it is often difficult to encourage people to think about what they are learning. It is the activity that is the central object of their attention. This is an expression of the classic tension between process and product which has been the subject of some debate within both youth work and community work (M. Smith, 1982: 6–7). Reflection and theory-making are left to the individual and the gains are made smaller than they might be had attention be paid to competences in, and commitment to, theory-making.

In sum, informal education could be said to have the following characteristics:

1 It can take place in a variety of settings, many of which are used for other, non-educational, purposes.
2 The process is deliberate and purposeful in that the people concerned are seeking to acquire some knowledge, skills and/or attitudes. However, such purpose and intent may not always be marked by closely specified goals.
3 Timescales are likely to be highly variable and often structured by the dynamics of the particular institution(s) in which exchanges are set. Most of those institutions will not primarily be concerned with education.
4 Participation is voluntary and is often self-generated.
5 The process is dialogical and marked by mutual respect.
6 There will be an active appreciation of, and engagement with, the social systems through which participants operate, and the cultural forms they utilize.

7 It may use both experiential and assimilated information patterns of learning.

When set against the characteristics of formal education, the contrasts are apparent. Formal education will tend to take place in a 'sole-use' setting, possess a more explicit and codified curriculum, exhibit different forms of time structuring, participation may or may not be voluntary, processes may or may not be dialogical, and there may not be an active appreciation of the participants' cultures and social networks. However, we should not fall into the trap of seeing these forms as polar opposites. They are more akin to traditions of thinking. Nor should we regard one tradition as being superior to the other. They contain elements which are appropriate to specific situations and could be seen as complementary to one another. The obvious slippage that can occur when considering these, is the simple equation with classical and romantic notions of education:

Classical	Romantic
Subject-centred	Child-centred
Skills	Creativity
Instruction	Experience
Information	Discovery
Obedience	Awareness
Conformity	Originality
Discipline	Freedom

(Lawton, 1975: 22)

It can be quickly seen from this listing that particular formal and informal educational initiatives could be expressive of either of the two ideal types. However, it is probably true that educators with a more romantic view have been drawn to informal approaches and, as such, have tended to put form before content (Yarnitt, 1980). Linked with this has been an assumption that in some way a concern with process and the so-called romantic curriculum is more radical, more likely to achieve social change. That view is disputed here. First, pedagogic method is secondary to the overall purpose of education. Secondly:

Education aiming to promote the eradication of class division must include, at the very least, some old-fashioned instruction, set into an ordered curriculum, which includes basic information and skills required to execute necessary management tasks. (Lovett *et al.*, 1983: 144)

Furthermore, each person must be able to 'analyse and think on a par with those intellectual traditions he must overcome in order to take up his proper place in civil and political society' (Gramsci, quoted in Stone, 1981: 241) and such learning is often based upon 'tedious rote learning of a whole intellectual tradition' (ibid.). For this reason it is essential to pay due regard to direction and content in any conceptualization of informal education we may care to advance and recognize that an over-reliance upon informal educational methods can actively disable those involved. Just as a focus on enlarging people's understanding of well-being and developing their civic courage is just one aspect of the educational task, so informal education is just one element of the process.

Critical dialogue

One of the key points of orientation for informal educators is the quality of dialogue that exists in the settings where they work. By helping to create and maintain the conditions and context for dialogue, educators are performing an essential part of their task. The importance of this has been recognized by many youth workers, but often in a somewhat under-theorized way. For example, when exploring the social and leisure traditions of youth work, it was seen that workers used notions such as 'there was a real buzz' or 'people were really talking' when asked how they judge whether a session had been 'good'. What features in these judgements is a concern with the nature and experience of communication. Often there is an interest in content, that people are 'talking about things that really matter'. However, these ideas require rigorous examination.

In everyday usage, dialogue is usually taken to mean something rather more than conversation. It suggests a note of seriousness. For example, in the traditional political arena, the word is often used to denote the exchanges between parties prior to formal negotiation. For the informal educator, five important elements require attention. First, dialogue implies a shared focus. A characteristic of many conversations is that they are often, in reality, separate monologues. The participants have their own themes which they develop as the conversation continues, but the subjects may never meet. Hence, dialogue entails some agreement about what is actually to be talked about, and adherence to this by those involved.

Secondly, dialogue presupposes listening, thinking and talking. It assumes that that participants make an effort to hear what is being said, attempt to understand it and apply their critical faculties before responding. This is not simply the application of a series of technical skills. In order to listen, and to engage genuinely in dialogue, participants must respect each other.

Thirdly, while we have been using the example of face-to-face spoken exchanges, dialogue can also exist when using the written word or symbols. Writing letters or communicating via electronic mail would be a reasonably responsive example of such a dialogue, but it could equally be the interaction of reader and writer. Similarly, the dialogue may only involve one person. Sometimes we say that reflection is the mind's conversation with itself. 'If not explicitly in language, at least we must admit that this conversation prefigures language' (Kemmis, 1985: 143).

Fourthly, dialogue requires a language of some form. Language allows communication, social interaction, thought and control. It is a means of transmitting ideas and perceptions of experiences between individuals and provides a medium through which people can categorize, order and direct their experiences, understandings, and relations with other people. These functions do not operate independently.

> Individuals come to recognize the ways in which others communicate – the linguistic rules they seem to obey, the styles to which they conform, and the particular symbols they employ to describe the world and to order their knowledge of it. In learning how to use these practices for their own purposes, they internalize certain representations created by other people which can be used in the formulation of their own understandings and interpretations of the world. (Walker and Meighan, 1981: 133)

In this way, the language environment in which people are engaged will come to influence both how people communicate with others and how they conceptualize and think. The informal educator has, therefore, to pay special attention to words and symbols and their context.

Fifthly, the informal educator must be concerned with praxis:

> Within the word we find two dimensions, reflection and action, in such radical interaction that if one is sacrificed – even in part – the other immediately suffers. There is no true word that is not at the same time a praxis. Thus, to speak a true word is to transform the world' (Freire, 1972: 60).

Freire places a particular emphasis upon praxis, upon informed action and thinking occasioned by action:

The act of knowing involves a dialectical movement that goes from reflection upon action to a new action. For the learner to know what he did not know before, he must engage in an authentic process of abstraction by means of which he can reflect on the action-object whole, or, more generally, on forms of orientation in the world. (Freire, 1985: 50–51)

Goulet has described one of the basic components of Freire's work as 'participant observation of educators "tuning in" to the vocabular universe of the people' (1974: viii). However, 'tuning in' is only one element of a process which aims to problematize the historical and cultural reality in which people are immersed. Through dialogue with an educator people come to create a new understanding of words, one which is 'explicitly critical and aimed at action, wherein those who were formally illiterate now begin to reject their role as mere "objects" in nature and social history and undertake to become "subjects" of their own destiny' (Goulet, 1974). Instead of existing in a culture of silence and submission, learners are to be encouraged to be creators and to become autonomous.

Along with this laudatory emphasis upon process, two dangers are apparent in the romantic nature of Freire's work. First, there is a seeming disregard for content and direction. Here, Freire often appears to relapse into the 'maze of authenticity' (Lovett *et al.*, 1983: 142), of judging things by some largely rhetorical and non-empirical vision of the true-self. Secondly, there is a tendency towards collapsing the roles of educator and learner. I have already argued that it is necessary to recognize the distinctions between the roles. Even where there is 'self-education' there are two roles and a dialogue between them. In this formulation of informal education, the relationship is to be marked by mutual respect and this, in turn, is based upon the recognition of differences. The educator does possess certain forms or combinations of expertise which the learner, by and large, does not. This is not to deny that 'the relationship between teacher and pupil is active and reciprocal so that every teacher is always a pupil and every pupil a teacher' (Gramsci, 1971: 350). The learner certainly possesses other forms of expertise which are relevant to the enterprise and of worth to the educator, but this should not lead to the erroneous assumption that they are the same or necessarily of equal interest at that point in time.

The recognition of the significance of dialogue for the educator is of great importance. The relationship between educators and learners is brought into being through the use of forms of discourse and content which are rooted in the culture and experiences of the learners and 'made problematic through modes of critical dialogue' (Giroux, 1983: 228). This process of enabling ideas, attitudes and experiences to be viewed as problematic, as requiring questioning and analysis, is also directed towards action. Here the notion of praxis is essential, directing attention to the importance of informed action and theory which has a meaning in the world.

Informal education and problems with curriculum

While there is an air of immediacy about informal education practice, of the need to start with the concerns that are presented, this should not blind us to the amount of planning and structuring that is necessary for effective practice. It is often those very activities which appear most unstructured and reactive, which require substantial preparation and critical attention. An obvious example here is detached youth work, where workers would soon be dominated by the 'tyranny of structurelessness' (Freeman, 1975). Without the usual rhythms and imperatives of building-based work, it is necessary to have a clear sense of purpose and to establish patterns simply to survive, let alone to undertake effective work. The obvious label under which much of this structuring process could be addressed is 'the curriculum'; however, there are particular problems associated with this concept in the context of informal education.

There is, of course, a confusing range of definitions attached to 'curriculum'. In its original sense it could be understood to be 'the prescribed content' for study. Thus, a curriculum is not a syllabus, which rather suggests a detailed account of materials or resources to be used, nor a statement of aims, but an outline of the subject matter to be studied (Barrow, 1984: 3). However, much writing in the field of curriculum studies has tended to redirect attention from content. For instance, Stenhouse argues that the fundamental questions on which curriculum research and development can throw light on are questions of translating purpose into policy and trying to realize aspirations, whatever they may be (Stenhouse, 1975). This shift came about with a growing awareness of the range of extraneous factors that can make a substantial difference to how content is experienced and what is learnt. Terms like 'hidden curriculum' came into common usage and have been applied to an ambiguous range of concerns. As a result, Jackson (1971) talks of the three R's of rules, routines and regulations that must be learnt by pupils if they are to survive in the classroom; Holt (1969) describes a set of strategies called 'right answerism'; and Bowles and Gintis (1976) have analysed the social control aspects in terms of 'correspondence theory' where the attitudes inculcated by the school are said to correspond to those required to maintain the class-based system of production.

The problem with this extension of meaning is that it can become coterminous with 'education' and so lose use. As Barrow argues, it is easier to recognize that a curriculum, defined relatively narrowly in terms of content, may have unintended consequences, and then to explore that issue, than it is to be alert to all the conceivable ramifications of a broad concept (Barrow, 1984: 10). For discussion here, I have, therefore, taken Barrow's adaptation of Hirst's (1968) definition and view the curriculum as 'a programme of activities (by teachers and pupils) designed so that pupils will attain so far as possible certain educational and other schooling ends or objectives' (Barrow, 1984: 11). What this definition of curriculum does leave open is the way in which the content may be prescribed. It may take the form of named activities, situations to be experienced or, for example, specified subjects.

The literature of schooling has exhibited a longstanding concern with 'curriculum' while that of youth work and community work has not. The reasons for this are not hard to find. First, as such work is not usually linked to certification there has not been a need to work through a prescribed syllabus. In this sense content has been less to the fore. Secondly, as we noted in our earlier discussion of informal education, purpose and intention may not be marked by closely specified goals. Learning may be apparently haphazard and unsuccessful at times. Thirdly, 'education' is only one of a number of interlinking traditions that have informed the development of youth work and community work.

There have been those who have sought to encourage 'curriculum thinking' in these sectors (National Youth Bureau, 1975, 1983), but it is, in general, an unhelpful notion, as reflection on Barrow's definition demonstrates. Central to this consideration is the relative openendedness of both aim and method. It is a characteristic of informal education that exchanges are based around a broad set of aims or concerns within which objectives are formulated and reformulated as the learning project progresses. Such concerns and objectives arise from the dialogues involving educators and learners. Outcomes at any one point may not be marked with a high degree of specificity. The concerns that informal educators bring to their exchanges with young people may be to do with the subordination of girls and young women, the desire to empower the young, to give them an opportunity to enjoy themselves or the wish to see them gain the ability and confidence to organize things for themselves. Similarly, young people will bring another set of concerns which will need to overlap in some way if there is to be agreement about programme. It is misguided to call these sets of concerns or indeed the programme that results, a curriculum.

First, the level of prescription has to be 'low'. In such a fluid situation, the important element that educators and learners need to hold on to is the essential direction of their activities. Thus, while there may be a fundamental concern with content in the model of informal education presented here, this cannot approach the degree of specificity that might be expected in some more formal situations. Learners and educators are liable to alter the activities utilized as circumstances and feelings change. When a fair comes to town, youth workers may well close down their building and use the fairground as the site for their activities. Community workers will have to respond to rapid changes in the political, social and physical environment. At one point the concern of the people they work with may be heating bills, at another the closure of a school, at yet another changes in social security regulations. Some educators will be able to describe and utilize a detailed programme of activities that could approximate to a curriculum. To do so they would have to create and maintain a working environment that controls and limits the extent to which the changing concerns of those they work with are brought into the process. In other words, they will have to sacrifice a degree of 'responsiveness' when attempting to take people's current concerns and work with them. While this is clearly important and necessary in a large number of cases, it does alter the nature of the enterprise.

Secondly, there is a rather more pragmatic set of reasons for wishing to avoid the notion of curriculum (as against content). Not only has the notion of curriculum been the subject of definitional debate and somewhat loose usage, but it is very much the property of formalized education. It is steeped in that tradition. Thus, while informal educators must rightly be encouraged to pay attention to content, to express that concern within the language of curriculum is to invite forms of thinking that do not necessarily resonate with informal traditions and the realities of practice. It is important to find a way of expressing the notion of prescribed content, that both links with the language of informal education, and that recognizes the essential differences with formalized education. The way in which the notion of curriculum has been imported tends not to meet these requirements. Indeed, it can all too easily amount to the colonization of a particular educational form by the proponents of another.

If the notion of curriculum is problematic, and significance is attached to content, then some other way of conceptualizing this dimension is necessary. Here I have portrayed content at two levels. First, it is necessary for educators and learners to have an idea of the *direction* in which they wish to go. Thus, educators may bring, for example, a range of concerns about enabling the collective advance of black people or the development of an enhanced understanding of well-being. Given the fluidity of informal education, it is essential that direction or essential purpose is a constant point of reference, both for the learner and the educator. Indeed, it is likely to be a source of tension and debate between both educators and learners and within these 'groupings'. Secondly, on a day-to-day level, the concern with direction and purpose should lead to a focus upon *topic*, the actual subject under discussion or investigation. The question here being what the relationship of the particular subject matter is to the concerns of those involved.

In practice, the consideration of direction and topic is an essential prerequisite of any thinking about method. The nature of the topic will have serious implications for the structuring of the learning environment and the means adopted. Similarly, it is likely that the intended direction of learning will predispose people to particular ways of proceeding.

In conclusion

Dewey concluded that 'one of the weightiest problems with which the philosophy of education has to cope is the method of keeping a proper balance between the informal and the formal, the incidental and the intentional modes of education' (1916: 9). The assumption that informal education is not an intentional mode has been disputed here. Indeed, it has been argued that informal education is a distinctive method which can be utilized in a range of social settings. Characterized by the central place accorded to critical dialogue, the stress laid upon engagement with learners' culture and the social systems through which they live their lives, the variety of settings that are utilized and the voluntary participation of learners, the notion of informal education would appear to offer youth work practitioners a useful means of thinking about method.

Chapter 8

Developing Popular Practice

Such is the organization of youth work that major advances can be made at the front-line in a relatively short time. The significant, initial questions concern strength of will and the way practitioners think. Once workers possess a sense of themselves as educators and grasp the dialogical nature of their task, then practice for the good can flow. In this chapter I will draw together some key considerations when approaching such practice.

The potential of popular practice

Popular youth work is the central site for the development of practice for the good. A recognition of this implies a substantial shift in emphasis, and the development of work with many groups of people who had not previously understood themselves as youth workers or educators. As Garrett discovered in her survey of provision for young people in Croydon (1986), for every group known to the Youth Service, there was at least one other who could equally be considered as undertaking youth work. In addition, there is a range of communal youth provision in the form of hobbyist and other clubs which, while not necessarily needing or welcoming youth work interventions, would benefit from certain forms of additional support. Their potential contribution to well-being very much parallels that of popular youth work.

As popular youth work is among the most pervasive forms of informal provision, this is where work must be focused. There is little political purpose in creating an oasis of positive work in some marginal area when it is attention to mass practice that is required. If, for example, familiar forms of work cannot be approached then there must be some questions about the ideological soundness of the proposal.

Secondly, given their appeal to the popular, these forms hold and reflect many contradictions and tensions in such a way as to make for the possibility of practice which addresses the lived experiences of the mass of young people. Specifically, in order to attract people, popular youth work has to make some accommodation with their culture. In that culture lies significant mechanisms of subordination and empowerment. The taken-for-granted and consciously learned can be subjected to critical interrogation, considered in relation to the good, so that people may own what they choose and attempt to transform that which does not fit their enlarged sense of well-being.

Thirdly, the organizational structure of much popular youth work is associational. Front-line units are usually organizations in themselves, possessing their own legal and financial status and having elected officials. Their structures at least make for the possibility of empowering practice. In addition, such organizations are part of formal political systems and can provide another doorway into collective political activity. These systems may connect directly with the local and central state; operate through federations, such as is the case with many sporting and hobby clubs and tenants associations; or work through other organizational structures, such as those present in churches. Further, some forms of youth provision are forms of mutual aid. The values and practices implicit within such groupings are of particular relevance to the purposes set for youth work in Chapter 6.

Fourthly, popular practitioners are frequently of the same neighbourhood or culture as those they work with. Therein lies the potential for organic practice, one that grows from within. In particular, it offers an opportunity for young people to work with people with whom they may share significant experiences, histories and prospects. If these people are able to demonstrate autonomy, an enlarged concern for people's well-being, and civic courage, then they are living evidence of what is actually possible. However, there are dangers. Practitioners may have either adopted the ways of bourgeois improvement or failed to make the familiar strange. Too much may be assumed because workers 'know' the community and culture.

Finally, the size and nature of popular youth work, characterized as it usually is by convivial and face-to-face relationships, allows for sustained dialogue. Whether, for example, the youth organization is large or small, there are usually a similar number of young people directly involved in organizing. If the aim of the work is partly to develop such competencies then the use of 'small' organizations makes sense. Further, it is important to examine the actual nature of relationships before assuming that so-called 'activity-clubs' are any less social than, say, the open youth club. In many enthusiast groupings the substantive activity may be of secondary importance when compared to the opportunities they provide for making friends and meeting people (see Chapter 3).

How, then, is practice to be transformed? The answer given here is that practice for the good is already within people's grasp, and that there is considerable potential within much popular youth work and communal youth provision once people start asking the right questions. But that is easier said than done. The dull compulsions of existing practice can conspire against critical reflection and dialogue. Nevertheless, those who want change can make progress by drawing upon the existing strengths of popular work, particularly if they are clear about purpose at a time when others are not.

Attention to identity and purpose

Practice for the good requires deep attention to the ways practitioners understand and name themselves. The term 'educator' makes many youth workers uncomfortable, its erroneous equation with classroom activity and discipline neither fitting practitioners' images of themselves, nor what they believe young people expect of their services. However, unless workers name themselves unambiguously they will remain forever locked in trivial pursuits.

Establishing a coherent identity as an educator does not come easy. Those who come to the work through their membership of a social movement will often be disposed to a view of themselves as educators, although they may also appeal to equally strong images such as proselytizer or organizer. They will, perhaps, be surer in their belief that they have something significant and distinctive to offer. The same may well be true of those who are concerned about young people through their involvement in communal leisure groups. For example, youthful entrants to a handball club or fishing club have to serve an apprenticeship while they 'learn the ropes', and require help in this.

The development and maintenance of people's identities as educators can be approached through training. None the less, it is sustained reflection and dialogue over time which provides the most potential, especially where this is based upon the exploration of actual and continuing practice and the traditions which it expresses. It is essential that things are not taken at their face value and that the hidden structures are sought; the underlying reasons for inter-vention require careful thought. One of the obvious forums for this process is the staff team or committee, another is individual super-vision (see Christian and Kitto, 1987).

A particular danger here is that people may be encouraged to take on ways of working that serve neither their interests, nor those they work with. This can happen as people adopt what are apparently the technical concerns of the professional without directly addressing what the cultural and political implications of these may be. The aim in this approach is to increase the number and effectiveness of popular educators committed to enlarging people's understanding of well-being, not to further the influence of bourgeois improvers, nor professionalize the area. In Gramsci's words this means working to produce '*elites* of intellectuals of a new type which arise directly out of the masses, but remain in contact with them to become, as it were, the whalebone in the corset' (1971: 340). To guard against the dangers of incorporation, practitioners must advance and own their political and moral understandings and identities as well as paying attention to their craft. As educators they must be educated. They too, must pursue their own well-being autonomously.

Beyond questions of identity lies attention to purpose and the need to stay close to fundamentals. Much in the same way as the family motto of Clarkes the shoemaker is supposedly 'But will it sell shoes?' (Goldsmith and Clutterbuck, 1985: 10), so practitioners must formulate their own essential question. One possibility here might be, 'But will it enable young people to pursue their own well-being autonomously?' More specifically, 'will it enlarge understanding of well-being or enhance ability to think and act politically?' Every action workers then take must be explainable in terms of this pur-pose. If the action does not fit then it is a diversion. Through this simple device many practitioners have generated a sureness of touch and direction which initially seemed impossible. But it is important to get the question right, and to tailor the process to the culture of the group. There are considerable dangers in applying concepts that make sense in the business world to the experiences of youth organizations and communal leisure groups. For example, in the case of the latter, there is the ever-present danger of focusing on the substantive activity of, say, football, rather than the social relations involved.

Tuning in

Workers must connect with the culture and language of those

worked with, as well as with their own, if they are to help people to appropriate their own biographies and develop understandings which are both true to their selves and the contexts in which they find themselves. This requires that particular attention is placed on the everyday, the apparently taken-for-granted: the material that people use to construct their view of the world and themselves. Attention to these matters is also of importance in furthering relations between those worked with:

> Just as, in their attempts to understand and describe other cultures, anthropologists and sociologists trip up over the concealed obstacles of cultural difference, so too do 'ordinary' people in their perception of and interaction with others. (Cohen, 1985: 39)

In true ethnographic fashion tuning-in involves worker-educators becoming 'strangers in their own land' or making the familiar strange. They have to look upon the everyday as if it was new. Some help in engaging in this process may be gained from the experience of researchers (see Ball, 1981; Whyte, 1955; Woods, 1979) and the various ethnographic 'cookbooks' (see Burgess, 1984; Hammersley and Atkinson, 1983; Hopkins, 1985; Spradley, 1979, 1980). However, it is likely that most will be gained from reflection on practice. Constantly, practitioners must pose questions about the settings in which they operate and the phenomena they encounter. Their own feelings and experiences can easily intrude in an unhelpful way. Workers may 'know' what it is like to be young and to grow up in a particular neighbourhood. This tendency to read in meanings does not allow for the fact that things change and that each individual experience is unique.

Unlike the ethnographer, to borrow from Marx (1977a: 158), the practitioner does not engage in the process simply to record the world in various ways, but to change it. Consciously assuming an attitude of naivety, of 'unknowingness', can encourage people both to explain and name their world, so that the worker-educator may understand. It can ensure active participation. In turn, practitioners have to pay special attention to the words used and check meanings. This not only displays respect for people, but also demonstrates the practitioner's reflective engagement with the world. Further, through this very naming and explaining, worker-educators can begin to gain a critical perspective on their own culture and history. While doing this it is important to remember that our capacity to mean what we intend to mean depends on the structure of the language we speak. Words have to be placed in context: the point of examining language is to explore the whole system within which speakers operate.

Working in this way requires clarity of purpose and the ability to explain succinctly and clearly what is being done. Time spent originating and refining such statements is rarely wasted. However fine the statement though, it will hardly guarantee entry to all groups or be acceptable to them. Workers should be especially alert to the process of entry into a group or setting. The responses to interventions, the negotiations necessary, and the roles adopted provides material which is of great relevance in developing and understanding practice and 'yields data on the ways in which different individuals perceive an organization or institution or neighbourhood' (Burgess, 1984: 49).

All of this further entails the constant monitoring of differences between practitioners and those with whom they work. This allows practitioners to stay rooted and yet maintain the necessary critical distance. It also provides an important context for the consideration of ethical questions. In the case of the latter, this may involve consideration of the sorts of activities and conversations worker-educators can be party to, e.g. in respect of acts which are outside the law or seriously contradict their ethical and political position.

Underpinning reflective activity is recording. To those not used to the disciplines of analytical thinking or who have not grasped the educational nature of their task, the effort involved in making notes about events and experiences often seems unnecessary or a luxury. However, there are few alternatives if practice is to be advanced. Reviewing such notes allows practitioners to see patterns emerging and to 'fix' the use of words. They provide a concrete means of exploring practice. In terms equally applicable to practitioners, Mills advocated the keeping of a journal in which there is joined:

> personal experience and professional activities, studies under way and studies planned. In this file, you, as an intellectual craftsman, will try to get together what you are doing intellectually and what you are experiencing as a person. Here you will not be afraid to use your experience and relate it directly to various work in progress. By serving as a check on repetitious work, your file also enables you to conserve your energy. It also encourages you to capture 'fringe-thoughts'. . . . Once noted, these may lead to more systematic thinking, as well as lend intellectual relevance to more directed experience. (Mills, 1970: 216–7)

Journals and records allow practitioners to evaluate events and phenomenon, they are storehouses of ideas which, when systematically approached, considerably enhance reflection and hence practice (Christian *et al.*, 1988; Rogers, 1982).

Tuning-in takes time and carries with it the danger that the bulk of worker-educators' efforts are spent on getting information for themselves, rather than working directly for the benefit of people. Within informal education the situation is compounded as much work is only of a relatively short duration. However, the problem here is less of time, than of disposition and orientation. If practitioners view the process as being simultaneously directed at their own entry into culture and at the development of a critical mode of reasoning in those they work with, then the necessary balance may be maintained.

Enabling dialogue, decision and learning

From what has already been said, it is apparent that worker-educators have at least three central working tasks, once they decide which broad areas they wish to handle and whom they want to work with. First, they contribute to the creation and maintenance of the conditions and context for dialogue. Secondly, they work with the learner(s) in order to reach agreement about the general direction of the required learning and specific topics of interest. In doing this they must ensure that all pay attention to what they are able and prepared to offer to the enterprise. Thirdly, practitioners make direct interventions to enable learning. When doing this they look to a range of sites for action. These include working:

(i)   directly with a group or individual;
(ii) with other people that the group or individual might consider significant, so influencing indirectly;
(iii) on the institution and systems which the group or individual experience;
(iv) on the physical environment or setting in which the work takes place; and
(v)   on the activities which the group or individuals undertake.

Differences in emphasis reflect, in part, the ideological position of the educator and learner and the direction and content of the learning. For example, within the character-building traditions, it can be seen that many workers tend to place an emphasis upon structure. They see their role as primarily providing a framework of activity and order. Badges, procedures, groupings like the 'six' and regular ritual provide a hierarchy of roles and activities through which young people must progress. Perhaps it is the young person's engagement with these, rather than with the worker which enables learning. This might be contrasted with some of the work within the personal and social development traditions, where practitioners may spend considerable amounts of time working directly with individuals or small groups.

At this point it is also necessary to assemble some of the key elements that practitioners will need to consider when approaching their tasks in relation to enabling dialogue, decision and learning. When the view of informal education advanced here is set alongside the processes and practices of youth work, a number of headings emerge which would appear to have some importance when thinking about intervention. This rather pragmatic summarized check list is included in order to give some structure to thinking about practice. Key elements for consideration are:

Content: Clearly, the nature of the material that educators and learners want to address will have serious implications for the methods utilized and the forms of intervention that are appropriate. Some ideas are better communicated through reading or lecturing, others require the use of small groups or individual sessions.

Networks and structures: Educators and learners have to gain an understanding of the nature of the social systems in which they are enmeshed. Of particular importance here are the networks of personal relationships in which people are involved and the impact of particular structures, such as those involved in the school, club or setting.

Rules and norms: Without careful attention to the ways in which learners understand both their own rules and norms and those which operate, and which they have in effect 'helped' construct, in the settings where the work is taking place, it is all too easy for practitioners to make inappropriate interventions. Their understanding of specific words or actions may well be different from those they work with.

Settings: As almost any introductory youth work text will unfailingly point out, the nature of the physical environment is of great importance. Does it make for creative interaction? Temperature, decoration, lighting, layout and furniture all seen to make an impact.

Activities: Here again we might examine particular activities for the degree to which they encourage interaction and attention to desired content. From this we might come away with pretty obvious conclusions such as noisy activities or pursuits involving a great deal of movement not being conducive to conversation. At a more sophisticated level practitioners must examine the differences in outcome involved in social conversations in a coffee bar and, say, in situations where both educator and learners are engaged in some structured tasks much as decorating 'their' youth club.

Attitudes: The disposition of those involved inevitably has an effect upon the learning that can be generated. As has already been stressed, mutual respect is of crucial importance. For practitioners this will manifest itself in a readiness to listen, think about what they have heard, ask relevant questions and make contributions that 'speak to the person's condition'.

Numbers: Frequent reference is made to size in discussions of youth work. Partly this arises from questions of economic viability, but it is also crucial in relation to the headings already listed. Physical settings may require a certain number in order that they may be experienced as convivial.

Time: Particular forms of organization, setting and activity are conducive to long-term work (such as the youth club), though many are not. Indeed, short-term work is often associated with informal education, e.g. the evening session or a particular discussion. In this respect, it is necessary to tailor activities not only to the time-span involved, but also to the gaps and disjunctures that can occur in informal practice.

It has not been possible to go into any depth concerning these elements where; however, while each element appears obvious, handling and combining the elements can require quite sophisticated practice (see Jeffs and Smith, forthcoming).

Asking 'what are people learning here?'

Immersion in the daily round and coping with the various tasks necessary to keep an organization going can easily lead to drift. In addition, because this form of learning often means people are engaged in doing things, whether it is organizing an evening's entertainment, campaigning against cuts in services or raising money to combat poverty, the direct objectives associated with these tasks can easily take precedence over the learning that is gained from the processes. The direction of the work can alter in ways unseen to practitioners and young people. It may be necessary to pull the work around so that it remains close to fundamentals. On the other hand, immediate objectives may have to be reformulated because the drift has arisen from an intuitive appreciation of changing needs. Asking 'what are people learning here?' keeps attention focused upon purpose and allows comparison with what people have identified as their learning requirements. Crucially this is a question that both practitioners and young people should be asking. The extent to which young people are considering this question is a good indicator of how successful the club or group is as an educational institution.

Aside from combating drift, the question also directs attention to theory-making. The very informality of the approach can deteriorate into superficiality with inadequate attention being paid to reflection: returning to experience, attending to feelings, and re-evaluating experience (Boud *et al.*, 1985: 26–36); and to the process of making and re-making theory. In the end it is theory which allows people to name, predict and act. The upshot of this for practitioners is that they will have to move beyond asking questions which elicit a simple descriptive response. As well as asking 'what happened?' or 'what is that?' they will have to focus attention on the relationship between things. 'How' and 'why' questions and considerations will have to feature in their repertoire. They will also have to direct people towards likely sources of theory and this may lead them into the adoption of more formalized teaching approaches at times.

Workers and mutual aid

This approach is dependent upon enabling young people to take responsibility for their own learning. It is they who are at the centre of the process. Therefore, practitioners must establish and maintain clear boundaries, resist pressures to take on what is not theirs, and control their own wishes and needs. Autonomy is not a thing to be conferred by others but is a way of behaving:

> We would tend to speak not of 'having autonomy' but of 'behaving autonomously'. Thus we do not see autonomy as a thing that can be taught, although it has to be learned. Autonomy is an attribute of relationship; to be non-autonomous is to be directed by another to whom one has handed over responsibility for choice and who is blamed if things go wrong and idealised if things go right. (Kitto, 1987: 67–8)

How then do young people learn to be autonomous in the context of a youth organization? The answer is that it has to be held and demonstrated as a value by the worker-educators and expressed in the structures.

The ability of practitioners to function effectively in this respect is dependent upon their being seen as different from those that they work with. They fulfil a distinctive function and in order to do so must ensure that the boundaries of their role are understood, and that they have established the necessary 'distance' between themselves and others. The problem with this is that if they are too distant, practitioners will experience considerable difficulties in functioning. Therefore, they have to search for the optimum point where their role as worker-educator is understood and accepted by all parties, and where they can establish relationships primarily in that role, rather than as a friend, neighbour or surrogate relative. They may indeed be these things at other times, but when these intrude into the arena of practice, confusions and defective interventions can occur.

Learning can also be deeply obstructed by workers stepping outside their role. People are not helped by workers who rush to put things right, who provide so much activity and undertake such tasks as to deny the opportunity for self-organization, or who seek to protect young people from engagement with wider political systems (Smith, 1984: 22). Central to the approach advocated here is the creation and use of opportunities for young people to organize things for themselves. These groupings, having their own integrity and their own products which, by and large, are consumed by themselves, may be called mutual aid organizations (Bishop and Hoggett, 1986: 40). Such groupings can assume a variety of forms which only rarely involves the fully participatory model of maximum involvement of all members in decisions:

> Even if the organizers are returned unopposed to their posts year after year, there is a crucial difference between the nature of the organizations they run and those typical of, say, the voluntary welfare sector. The essential difference lies in the way in which the members perceive the organizers. Is the organization done 'by some of us, for all of us' or is it performed 'by them, for us'? . . .
>
> The key point . . . is not that these two different perceptions hide otherwise similar relationships, but that the very quality of relations between members of any mutual aid group is one of a crucially different nature. The basis of mutual aid is reciprocity, to the extent that relationships – essentially the exchange of effort and involvement – are governed by a very loose concept of 'give and take'. (Bishop and Hoggett, 1986: 41)

Not only do such organizational forms accord with the central tasks advocated here for youth work, but they also provide a rare if not unique opportunity to 'reassert values related not to passive consumerism but to production for one's own use and enjoyment' (Bishop and Hoggett, 1986: 44).

This emphasis upon mutual aid and the importance of worker-educators identifying and operating within appropriate boundaries means that they have to be vigilant about the roles they perform. In concrete terms this probably means that they will have to perform three main roles.

First, they will often have to act as *managers* of a particular piece of plant. This can result in an all too familiar story as the building takes over and is perceived as the worker's property (Stone, 1987). Such responsibilities cannot be denied but they can be managed in a different way. For example, like the manager of a public hall, they can establish a contract with users. In return for payment and the adherence to certain rules, young people have use of the plant. But this is not an individualized contract. The users have to be organized in some body so that they may act collectively and be 'hirers' and organizers themselves. This, in turn, provides a context for many of the central tasks of youth work to be performed.

Where practitioners are not direct providers of premises, e.g. where a group meets in a village hall, the formal organization of young people may make a contract with the hall committee in much the same way. If this is not possible then the workers will have to adopt an intermediary role, on the one hand making a contract with the hall committee, on the other with the young people.

Secondly, practitioners will act as *informal educators* with groups and individuals. In this approach, it is young people who have the responsibility for framing rules, organizing programmes and carrying out activities. The young people involved may wish to call upon the services of worker-educators so that they may develop the necessary competencies and dispositions. They may also require basic information concerning, for example, the availability and scope of local authority or voluntary organizations' services. Where 'organized' groups do not exist, but where there is some wish to 'do something', the worker-educator is likely to have to spend considerable time working with individuals and small groups in order that they may set themselves up so that they might use provision and develop programmes (see Lacey, 1987).

As well as acting as a consultant concerning the organization and running of the group, practitioners will usually want to offer their services generally as informal educators to those who use the provision. To do this they will have to get the agreement of the young people's organization so that they may operate in this way.

Thirdly, practitioners may indeed make available certain direct forms of provision and opportunities for learning where they take ultimate responsibility. This may be because they need to provide an initial point of reference for people. For example, there is now evidence that young women are making increasing use of more structured youth provision such as that offered by schools and Duke of Edinburgh's Award Schemes rather than of 'open' youth provision (Jeffs and Smith, 1988a: 127). The reasons for this are not difficult to find. In such activities, the structures provide a degree of predictability, people know what to expect; they guarantee space, which is not so likely to be crowded out by young men; they allow the development of particular interests; and they are seen as legitimate, in particular, by parents. Workers may well have to provide structured activities in this way, but they must also ensure that they do so in such a way as to allow people to move on; i.e. that structures exist through which young people can take responsibility and 'organize around enthusiasms' (Bishop and Hoggett, 1986).

In this role as *organizing educator*, practitioners must ensure that their activities are clearly separated from those organized by young people. For example, they may want to put on a specific course or series of sessions or organize a training weekend around a particular theme. When doing so it is vital that they make a careful estimate of how this will effect the group. It may act as a discouragement to the group to organize and, if the scale of the provision is substantial, may contradict the core purpose. Direct provision of programmes by practitioners is, thus, something to be deeply suspicious of. While there may be a case for short-term or discreet provision by worker-educators, a careful limit must be placed on such activities. Having established that the practitioner's task is concerned with the development and maintenance of the context for dialogue, decision and learning, it is perhaps easier to say 'no' to requests for them to organize all sorts of other activities.

Policy implications

While not expecting vast numbers of policy makers to be disposed towards the political direction of these proposals, it is worth outlining briefly some obvious considerations in constructing broad programmes for the good.

First and foremost, it must be recognized that the locus for change lies in the front line, in the dialogue between young people and workers, and workers and workers. This is where resources must be deployed. Further, policy construction must be driven by the lessons of reflective practice. It is likely that very different sets of demands will be made on the administrative framework and upon specialist services such as training as popular practice develops. But the exact shape of those demands is unclear and it is therefore foolish to attempt grand designs. Rather policy and structure must grow organically with practice.·

Secondly, at the front line, resources have to be deployed in a way which promotes dialogue, critical engagement and political con-sciousness. Localized or movement-connected, small-scale and con-vivial youth work would appear to offer the most appropriate opportunity for this. Youth or neighbourhood houses, village clubs, enthusiast clubs, groupings associated with community organiza-tion provision, self-organized interest groups and small informal groupings of young people, wherever they are found, would all appear to be possible sites for practice for the good. It is also possible to create little islands of dialogical practice within large-scale pro-duct-focused provision, such as that associated with sport and recreation, but the actual activity provision should be left to others. Wherever possible workers should not be deployed in the manage-ment of large-scale plant, but should be engaged directly in work with either young people or with those that work with them. In other words, it is necessary to assert that practitioners are educators rather than leisure managers or coordinators. Large-scale activity pro-vision should be located within schools and leisure departments; substantial and complex plant should either go the same way or the management be given over to community associations and the like.

Any relevant strategy must ensure proper staffing levels, payment rates and conditions of employment for the mass of part-timers who constitute the labour force (Harper, 1985; Callow, 1983). Further, workers (both full- and part-time) must be given greatly enlarged opportunities to develop critical practice. This not only implies the development of substantial programmes to enable reflection and theory-making, but also the allocation of resources for proper pay-ment for attendance at training courses, staff meetings and work-shops. Such programmes must not be restricted to the interrogation and explanation of practice, they must enter into the wider phil-osophical and political concerns that should be paramount when considering purpose and direction.

One obvious response could be to redeploy full-time workers into area 'support' roles, but this could be mistaken given that the bulk of such workers have not demonstrated that they are versed in the sort of dialogical, empowering practice advocated here. For this reason it is essential that full-time workers undertake sustained and substantial face-to-face work and interrogate it. This is aside from any consideration of the lack of productivity of such 'support' roles when compared to direct work with young people (Jeffs and Smith, 1988a), or that working alongside part-timers might be the most effective means of enabling them to develop their practice in the imperfect circumstances in which they find themselves. Many workers are not in the position to devote long periods to 'off-the-job' training.

Thirdly, such a strategy would also benefit from practitioners being located within an administrative context which has education unambiguously as its primary focus. Unfortunately, this cannot be said of the existing Youth Service and increasingly seems unlikely given the growing organizational diversity outlined in Chapter 4. As a consequence, practitioners will have to spend a considerable amount of time in securing administrative and managerial understandings and practices which complement the work.

Amidst the centralizing and controlling tendencies of the late 1980s, a plea for organic policy-making looks distinctly utopian, but the localized and diverse structures of youth work still allow for a high degree of discretion at the front-line. Indeed, there are major structural constraints on the extent to which such work can be centrally directed (Jeffs and Smith, 1988a). Other of these proposals may occur as the result of shifts in youth policy towards policing, skilling and leisurism and the failure of key forms of youth work to deliver what is expected of them. In a similar fashion, dialogical approaches may be appropriated and reinterpreted in the interests of bourgeois improvement. Well-being can easily be understood in a narrow, selfish and individualistic manner, as the politics of the 1980s sadly demonstrates. Luckily, the traditions of practice which strive to move forward in another direction have continued to evolve. Many of the elements of practice for good are tantalizingly close to hand – they are part of everyday experience. All that is needed is their informed and critical use. But realizing this potential in any substantial way requires major shifts in the way many youth workers organize their world. This is not easy when books have to be balanced at the end of the day, when much of the discussion about youth work is rhetorical, and when so many youth workers have an interest in encouraging the mass of young people to accept their lot stoically. Not easy, but still possible.

Bibliography

Abercrombie, A. and Turner, B.S. (1982). 'The Dominant Ideology Thesis', in Giddens, A. and Held, D. (eds). *Classes, Power and Conflict*. London, Macmillan.

Adams, R. (1988). 'Finding a way in. Youth workers and juvenile justice', in Jeffs. T. and Smith, M. (eds). *Welfare and Youth Work Practice*. London, Macmillan (in press).

Adams, R. *et al.* (1981). *A Measure of Diversion?* Leicester, National Youth Bureau.

Allbeson, J. (1985). 'Seen but not heard: young people', in Ward, S. (ed.). *DHSS in Crisis*. London, Child Poverty Action Group.

Allen, G. *et al.* (eds) (1987). *Community Education: Agenda for Educational Reform*. Milton Keynes, Open University Press.

Aries, P. (1962). *Centuries of Childhood*. London, Jonathan Cape.

BYV Social Education Project (1981). *Working Together. The Use of Social Education Techniques in the Secondary School Form Period*. Birmingham, Birmingham Young Volunteers.

Bacon, R. and Eltis, W. (1976). *Britain's Economic Problems: Too Few Producers*. London, Macmillan.

Bailey, P. (1987). *Leisure and Class in Victorian England. Rational Recreation and the Contest for Control 1830–1885* (2nd edn). London, Methuen.

Baker, S.H. (1919). *Character Building for Boys. The Scientific Management of Clubs for Boys*. London, YMCA Boys Department.

Baldwin, J. and Wells, H. (eds) (1979–81). *Active Tutorial Work. Books 1–5*. Oxford, Blackwell.

Ball, S.J. (1981). *Beachside Comprehensive. A Case Study of Secondary Schooling*. Cambridge, Cambridge University Press.

Barnes, L.J. (1945). *Youth Service in an English County*. London, King George's Jubilee Trust.

Barnes, L.J. (1948). *The Outlook for Youth Work*. London, King George's Jubilee Trust.

Barrow, R. (1984). *Giving Teaching Back to the Teachers. A Critical Introduction to Curriculum Theory*. Brighton, Wheatsheaf Books.

Bennett, T. (1986a). 'Introduction: Popular culture and "the turn to Gramsci" ', in Bennett, T. *et al.* (eds). *Popular Culture and Social Relations*. Milton Keynes, Open University Press.

Bennett, T. (1986b). 'The politics of the "popular" & popular culture', in Bennett, T. *et al.* (eds). *Popular Culture and Social Relations*. Milton Keynes, Open University Press.

Best, G. (1979). *Mid-Victorian Britain 1851-75*. London, Fontana.

Bharati, A. (1985). 'The self in Hindu thought and action', in Marsella, A.J. *et al.* (eds). *Culture and Self. Asian and western perspectives*. London, Tavistock.

Binfield, C. (1973). *George Williams and the YMCA. A Study in Victorian Social Attitudes*. London, Heinemann.

Bishop, J. and Hoggett, P. (1986). *Organizing Around Enthusiasms. Mutual Aid in Leisure*. London, Comedia.

Blackburn, D. (1988). 'Youth work and disability', in Jeffs, T. and Smith, M. (eds). *Welfare and Youth Work Practice*. London, Macmillan (in press).

Blanch, M. (1979). 'Imperialism, nationalism and organized youth', in Clarke, J. *et al.* (eds). *Working Class Culture*. London, Hutchinson.

Board of Education (1939). *In the Service of Youth (Circular 1486)*. London, HMSO.

Board of Education (1940). *The Challenge of Youth (Circular 1516)*. London, HMSO.

Board of Education (1941). *Circular 1577*. London, HMSO.

Board of Education (1944). *Teachers and Youth Leaders (The McNair Report)*. London, HMSO.

Bocock, R. (1986). *Hegemony*. London, Tavistock.

Bolger, S. and Scott, D. (1984). *Starting from Strengths*. Leicester, National Youth Bureau.

Bone, M. and Ross, E. (1972). *The Youth Service and Similar Provision for Young People*. London, HMSO.

Booton, F. (1980). 'Deschooling the Youth Service', in Booton, F. and Dearling, A. (eds). *The 1980s and Beyond*. Leicester, National Youth Bureau.

Booton, F. (ed.) (1985). *Studies in Social Education, Vol 1. 1860-1890*. Hove, Benfield Press.

Boud, D. *et al.* (eds) (1985). *Reflection. Turning Experience into Learning*. London, Kogan Page.

Bowles, S. and Gintis, H. (1976). *Schooling in Capitalist America*. London, Routledge and Kegan Paul.

Bray, R. (1907). *The Town Child*. London, Fisher Unwin.

Brew, J. Mac. (1943). *In the Service of Youth*. London, Faber.

Brew, J. Mac. (1946). *Informal Education. Adventures and Reflections*. London, Faber.

Brookfield, S. (1983). *Adult Learning, Adult Education and the Community*. Milton Keynes, Open University Press.

Brookfield, S.D. (1986). *Understanding and Facilitating Adult Learning.* Milton Keynes, Open University Press.

Brown, A. (1986). *Modern Political Philosophy. Theories of the Just Society.* Harmondsworth, Penguin.

Brown, C. (1986). 'Social education in secondary schools: principles and practice', in Brown, C. *et al.* (eds). *Social Education: Principle and Practice.* Lewes, Falmer Press.

Brown, C. *et al.* (eds) (1986). *Social Education: Principles and Practice.* Lewes, Falmer Press.

Bulmer, M. (1987). *The Social Basis of Community Care.* London, Allen and Unwin.

Bunt, S. (1975). *Jewish Youth Work in Britain. Past, Present, and Future.* London, Bedford Square Press.

Bunt, S. and Gargrave, R. (1980). *The Politics of Youth Clubs.* Leicester, National Youth Bureau.

Burgess, R.G. (1984). *In the Field. An Introduction to Field Research.* London, George Allen and Unwin.

Burley, D. (1980). *Issues in Community Service.* Leicester, National Youth Bureau.

Burley, D. (1982). *Starting Blocks – Aspects of Social Education Group Work with Young People.* Leicester, National Youth Bureau.

Butters, S. and Newell, S. (1978). *Realities of Training.* Leicester, National Youth Bureau.

Button, L. (1981). *Group Tutoring for the Form Teacher: Vol. 1. Lower Secondary School.* London, Hodder and Stoughton.

Button, L. (1982). *Group Tutoring for the Form Teacher: Vol. 2. Upper Secondary School.* London, Hodder and Stoughton.

CARF/Southall Rights (1981). *Southall – The Birth of a Black Community.* London, Institute of Race Relations.

Callow, F. (1983). 'A tradition of exploitation'. *Youth in Society*, 53.

Carey, S. and Shukur, A. (1986). 'A profile of the Bangladeshi community in East London'. *New Community*, XII (3).

Carpenter, V. and Young, K. (1986). *Coming in from the Margins. Youth Work with Girls and Young Women.* Leicester, National Association of Youth Clubs.

Christian, C. and Kitto, J. (1987). *The Theory and Practice of Supervision.* London, YMCA National College.

Christian, C. *et al.* (1988). *Issues in Supervision.* London, YMCA National College (in press).

Clarke, J. and Critcher, C. (1985). *The Devil Makes Work. Leisure in Capitalist Britain.* London, Macmillan.

Clarke, J. *et al.* (eds) (1979). *Working Class Culture. Studies in History and Theory.* London, Hutchinson.

Coffield, F. *et al.* (1986). *Growing Up at the Margins: Young Adults in the North East.* Milton Keynes, Open University Press.

Cohen, A.P. (1985). *The Symbolic Construction of Community.* London, Tavistock.

Cohen, P. (1984). 'Against the New Vocationalism', in Bates I. *et al.* (eds). *Schooling for the Dole: The New Vocationalism*. London, Macmillan.

Coleman, J.C. (1980). *The Nature of Adolescence*. London, Methuen.

Coleman, J.S. (1976). 'Differences between experiential and classroom learning', in Keeton, M.T. (ed.). *Experiential Learning*. San Francisco, Josey-Bass.

Coombs, P.H. *et al.* (1973). *New Paths to Learning*. New York, UNICEF.

Crick, B. and Porter, A. (eds) (1978). *Political Education and Political Literacy*. London, Longman.

Cunningham, H. (1980). *Leisure in the Industrial Revolution*. London, Croom Helm.

DES (1969). *Youth and Community Work in the 70's (The Fairbairn-Milson Report)*. London, HMSO.

DES (1983a). *Youth Service Provision in Two Areas of Bedfordshire. Report by HM Inspectors*. London, DES.

DES (1983b). *Young People in the 80's. A Survey*. London, HMSO.

DES (1986). *Aspects of the Work of the Youth Service in Wigan*. London, DES.

David, K. (1983). *Personal and Social Education in Secondary Schools*. York, Longman for the Schools Council.

Davidoff, L. (1976). 'The rationalization of housework', in Barker, D.L. and Allen, S. (eds). *Dependence and Exploitation in Work and Marriage*. Harlow, Longman.

Davies, B. (1986). *Threatening Youth. Towards a National Youth Policy*. Milton Keynes, Open University Press.

Davies, B. (1988). 'Professionalism or trade unionism', in Jeffs, T. and Smith, M. (eds). *Welfare and Youth Work Practice*. London, Macmillan (in press).

Davies, B. and Gibson, A. (1967). *The Social Education of the Adolescent*. London, University of London Press.

Dawes, F. (1975). *A Cry from the Streets. The Boys Club Movement in Britain*. Hove, Wayland.

DeVos, G. (1985). 'Dimensions of the self in Japanese culture', in Marsella, A.J. *et al.* (eds). *Culture and Self. Asian and Western Perspectives*. London, Tavistock.

DeVos, G., Marsella, A.J. and Hsu, F.L.K. (1985). 'Introduction', in Marsella, A.J. *et al.* (eds). *Culture and Self. Asian and Western Perspectives*. London, Tavistock.

Dewey, J. (1916). *Democracy and Education. An Introduction to the Philosophy of Education* (1966 edn). New York, Free Press.

Dewey, J. (1933). *How We Think* (revised edn). Boston, D.C. Heath.

Dewey, J. (1938). *Experience and Education* (1963 edn). New York, Macmillan.

Dick, M. (1980). 'The myth of the working class Sunday school'. *History of Education*, 9 (1).

Donald, J. (1985). 'Beacons of the future', in Beechey, V. and Donald, J.

(eds). *Subjectivity and Social Relations*. Milton Keynes, Open University Press.

Dyhouse, C. (1981). *Girls Growing Up in Late Victorian and Edwardian England*. London, Routledge and Kegan Paul.

Eagar, W. McG. (1953). *Making Men. A History of Boys' Clubs and Related Movements*. London, University of London Press.

Edwards-Rees, D. (1943). *The Service of Youth Book*. Wallington, Religious Education Press.

Eggleston, J. (1976). *Adolescence and Community. The Youth Service In Britain*. London, Edward Arnold.

Elliot, J. and Pring, R. (1975). 'Introduction', in Elliot, R. and Pring, R. (eds). *Social Education and Social Understanding*. London, University of London Press.

Entwistle, H. (1971). *Political Education in a Democracy*. London, Routledge and Kegan Paul.

Entwistle, H. (1981). 'The political education of adults', in Heater, D. and Gillespie, J.A. (eds). *Political Education in Flux*. London, Sage.

Evans, W.M. (1965). *Young People in Society*. Oxford, Blackwell.

Ewen, J. (1972). *Towards a Youth Policy*. Leicester, MBS Publications.

Finn, D. (1987). *Training without Jobs. New Deals and Broken Promises*. London, Macmillan.

Fordham, P. et al. (1979). *Learning Networks in Adult Education. Non-formal Education on a Housing Estate*. London, Routledge and Kegan Paul.

Foreman, A. (1987). 'Youth workers as redcoats', in Jeffs, T. and Smith, M. (eds). *Youth Work*. London, Macmillan.

Foster, J. (1977). *Class Struggle and the Industrial Revolution. Early Industrial Capitalism in Three English Towns*. London, Methuen.

Fraser, D. (1973). *The Evolution of the British Welfare State*. London, Macmillan.

Freeman, J. (1975). *The Tyranny of Structurelessness*. Kingston, Anarchist Workers Association.

Freire, P. (1972). *Pedagogy of the Oppressed*. Harmondsworth, Penguin.

Freire, P. (1974). *Education: The Practice of Freedom*. London, Writers and Readers Publishing Cooperative.

Freire, P. (1985). *The Politics of Education. Culture, Power and Liberation*. London, Macmillan.

Fryer, P. (1984). *Staying Power. The History of Black People in Britain*. London, Pluto Press.

Further Education Unit (1980). *Developing Social and Life Skills*. London, Further Education Unit.

Garrett, B. (1986). *1000 Links. Youth Activity in Croydon*. Croydon, Croydon Guild of Voluntary Organizations.

Giddens, A. (1979). *Central Problems in Social Theory*. London, Macmillan.

Giddens, A. (1984). *The Constitution of Society. Outline of the Theory of Structuration*. Cambridge, Polity Press.

Gillis, J.R. (1974, 1981). *Youth and History. Tradition and Change in*

European Age Relations 1770-Present. New York, Academic Press.

Gilroy, P. (1987). *There Ain't No Black in the Union Jack. The Cultural Politics of Race & Nation*. London, Hutchinson.

Giroux, H.A. (1983). *Theory and Resistance in Education*. London, Heinemann.

Gittins, D. (1985). *The Family in Question. Changing Households and Familiar Ideologies*. London, Macmillan.

Goetschius, G.W. and Tash, J. (1967). *Working with Unattached Youth. Problem, Approach, Method*. London, Routledge and Kegan Paul.

Goldsmith, W. and Clutterbuck, D. (1985). *The Winning Streak*. Harmondsworth, Penguin.

Goodman, P. (1960). *Growing Up Absurd*. London, Sphere Books.

Goodwin, B. (1982). *Using Political Ideas*. Chichester, John Wiley and Sons.

Gosden, P.H.J.H. (1976). *Education in the Second World War. A Study in Policy and Administration*. London, Methuen.

Gough, I. (1979). *The Political Economy of the Welfare State*. London, Macmillan.

Goulet, D. (1974). 'Introduction' to Freire, P., *Education: The Practice of Freedom*. London, Writers and Readers Publishing Cooperative.

Grafton, T. (1979). *No More Time. A Research Study of the Boot Night Shelter Project*. Leicester, National Youth Bureau.

Gramsci, A. (1971). *Selections from Prison Notebooks*. Edited and translated by Hoare, Q., Smith, G.N., London, Lawrence and Wishart.

Greenwood, J. (1869). *The Seven Curses of London. Scenes from the Victorian Underworld* (1981 edn). Oxford, Blackwell.

HMSO (1960). *The Youth Service in England and Wales (The Albemarle Report)*. London, HMSO.

HMSO (1982) *Experience and Participation. Report of the Review Group on the Youth Service in England (The Thompson Report)*. London, HMSO.

Hall, G.S. (1904). *Adolescence. Its Psychology, and Its Relation to Physiology, Anthropology, Sociology, Sex, Crime, Religion and Education*. New York, Appleton.

Hall, G.S. (1906). *Youth: Its Regime and Hygiene*. New York, Appleton.

Hall, S. and Schwarz, B (1985). 'State and society, 1880-1930', in Langan, M. and Schwarz, B. (eds). *Crises in the British State 1880-1930*. London, Hutchinson.

Hall, S., Lumley, B. and McLennan, G. (1978). 'Politics and ideology: Gramsci', in Centre for Contemporary Cultural Studies. *On Ideology*. London, Hutchinson.

Hammersley, M. and Atkinson, P. (1983). *Ethnography. Principles in Practice*. London, Tavistock.

Hanmer, J. (1964). *Girls at Leisure*. London, London Union of Youth Clubs.

Harper, B. (1983). *Better than Bessey? Training Provision for Part-time and Voluntary Youth Workers in the Statutory Sector in England and Wales*. Leicester, National Youth Bureau.

Harper, B. (1985). *People Who Count. Youth Work Resources in Local Authorities*. Leicester, National Youth Bureau.

Harris, R. and Seldon, A. (1979). *Over-Ruled on Welfare*. London, Institute of Economic Affairs.

Heller, A. (1976). 'Marx's theory of revolution and the revolution in every-day life', in Heller, A. *et al.* (eds). *The Humanization of Socialism. Writings of the Budapest School*. London, Alison and Busby.

Heller, A. (1983). *A Theory of History*. London, Routledge and Kegan Paul.

Heller, A. (1984). *Everyday Life*. London, Routledge and Kegan Paul.

Hemming, J. (1949). *The Teaching of Social Studies in Secondary Schools*. London, Longman.

Hendricks, H. (1986). 'Personality and psychology: defining Edwardian boys'. *Youth and Policy*, **18**.

Hendry, L.B. (1983). *Growing Up and Going Out. Adolescents and Leisure*. Aberdeen, Aberdeen University Press.

Hill, M. and Bramley, G. (1986). *Analysing Social Policy*. Oxford, Blackwell.

Hindess, B. (1987). *Freedom, Equality, and the Market. Arguments on Social Policy*. London, Tavistock.

Hirst, P.H. (1968). 'Contribution of philosophy to the study of the curriculum', in Kerr, J.F. (ed.). *Changing the Curriculum*. London, University of London Press.

Hobsbawm, E.J. (1968). *Labouring Men. Studies in the History of Labour*. London, Weidenfeld.

Hobsbawm, E. (1984). 'Introduction. Inventing traditions', in Hobsbawm, E. and Ranger, T. (eds). *The Invention of Tradition*. Cambridge, Cambridge University Press.

Holland, M. (1985). 'Education or leisure – whose move next?' *Youth in Society*, **103**.

Holt, J. (1969). *How Children Fail*. Harmondsworth, Penguin.

Hopkins, D. (1985). *A Teacher's Guide to Classroom Research*. Milton Keynes, Open University Press.

Hopson, B. and Scally, M. (1981). *Lifeskills Teaching*. London, McGraw Hill.

Houle, C.O. (1980). *Continuing Learning in the Professions*. San Francisco, Jossey-Bass.

Hudson, B. (1984). 'Femininity and adolescence', in McRobbie, A. and Nava, M. (eds). *Gender and Generation*. London, Macmillan.

Humphries, S. (1981). *Hooligans or Rebels? An Oral History of Working-class Childhood and Youth 1889–1939*. Oxford, Blackwell.

ILEA (1984). *The Youth Service. A Fair Deal for Girls?* London, ILEA.

ILEA (1986). *Social Education and Youth Work Practice. Towards More Conscious Practice and More Coherent Patterns of Provision*. London, ILEA.

Jackson, P. (1971). 'The student's world', in Silberman, M. (ed.). *The Experience of Schooling*. Eastbourne, Holt, Rinehart and Winston.

Jarvis, P. (1983a). *Professional Education*. London, Croom Helm.

Jarvis, P. (1983b). *Adult and Continuing Education. Theory and Practice*. London, Croom Helm.

Jarvis, P. (1985). *The Sociology of Adult and Continuing Education*. London, Croom Helm.

Jeffs, T. (1979). *Young People and the Youth Service*. London, Routledge and Kegan Paul.

Jeffs, T. and Smith, M. (eds) (1987a). *Youth Work*. London, Macmillan.

Jeffs, T. and Smith, M. (1987b). 'What future for initial training?' *Youth and Policy*, 20.

Jeffs, T. and Smith, M. (eds) (1988a). *Welfare and Youth Work Practice*. London, Macmillan (in press).

Jeffs, T. and Smith, M. (eds) (1988b). *Young People, Inequality and Youth Work*. London, Macmillan (in press).

Jeffs, T. and Smith, M. (forthcoming). *Informal Education. Theory and practice*.

Jensen, G. *et al.* (eds) (1964). *Adult Education: Outlines of an Emerging Field of University Study*. Washington, D.C., Adult Education Association of America.

John, G. (1981). *In the Service of Black Youth. The Political Culture of Youth and Community Work with Black People in English Cities*. Leicester, National Association of Youth Clubs.

Johnson, F. (1985). 'The Western concept of self', in Marsella, A.J. *et al.* (eds). *Culture and Self. Asian and Western Perspectives*. London, Tavistock.

Jones, C. (1983). *Social Work and the Working Class*. London, Macmillan.

Jones, K., Brown, J. and Bradshaw, J. (1983). *Issues in Social Policy*. London, Routledge and Kegan Paul.

Kemmis, S. (1985). 'Action research and the politics of reflection', in Boud, D. *et al.* (eds). *Reflection: Turning Experience into Learning*. London, Kogan Page.

Kent-Baguley, P. (1988). 'Youth work and sexuality', in Jeffs, T. and Smith, M. (eds). *Young People, Inequality and Youth Work*. London, Macmillan (in press).

Kett, J.F. (1977). *Rites of Passage: Adolescence in America, 1790 to the Present*. New York, Basic Books.

King George's Jubilee Trust (1951). *Youth Service To-morrow. A report of a meeting arranged by King George's Jubilee Trust and held at Ashridge 27–30 April 1951*. London, King George's Jubilee Trust.

Kitto, J. (1987). *Holding the Boundaries. Professional Training of Face to Face Workers at a Distance*. London, YMCA National College.

Kolb, D. (1976). *Learning Style Inventory*. New York, McBer and Co.

Kuper, B. (1985). 'The supply of training'. *Youth and Policy*, 13.

Lacey, F. (1987). 'Youth Workers as Community Workers', in Jeffs, T. and Smith, M. (eds). *Youth Work*. London, Macmillan.

Laqueur, T.W. (1976). *Religion and respectability: Sunday Schools and Working Class Culture*. New Haven, Yale University Press.

Law, I. (1981). *A History of Race and Racism in Liverpool, 1660–1950*. Liverpool, Merseyside Community Relations Council.

Lawson, K. (1974). 'Learning situations or educational situations', reprinted in Tight, M. (ed.) (1984). *Adult Learning and Education*. London, Croom Helm.

Lawton, A. (1984). *Youth Counselling Matters*. Leicester, National Youth Bureau.

Lawton, D. (1975). *Class, Culture and the Curriculum*. London, Routledge and Kegan Paul.

Le Grand, J. (1982). *The Strategy of Equality*. London, George Allen and Unwin.

Lee, R. (1980). *Beyond Coping*. London, Further Education Unit.

Leigh, M. and Smart, A. (1985). *Interpretation and Change. The Emerging Crisis of Purpose in Social Education*. Leicester, National Youth Bureau.

Leighton, J.P. (1972). *The Principles and Practice of Youth and Community Work*. London, Chester House.

Lewis, I.M. (1976). *Social Anthropology in Perspective. The Relevance of Social Anthropology*. Harmondsworth, Penguin.

Lindley, R. (1986). *Autonomy*. London, Macmillan.

Little, K.L. (1943). 'Colour prejudice in Britain'. *Wasu*, X (1).

Lovett, T. *et al.* (1983). *Adult Education and Community Action*. London, Croom Helm.

Mack, J. and Lansley, S. (1985). *Poor Britain*. London, George Allen and Unwin.

Mackie, J.L. (1977). *Ethics. Inventing Right and Wrong*. Harmondsworth, Penguin.

Macleod, D.I. (1983). *Building Character in the American Boy. Boy Scouts, YMCA & their Forerunners*. Madison, Wisconsin, University of Wisconsin Press.

Marsella, A.J. *et al.* (eds) (1985). *Culture and Self. Asian and Western Perspectives*. London, Tavistock.

Marsland, D. (1978). *Sociological Explorations in the Service of Youth*. Leicester, National Youth Bureau.

Marx, K. (1875). 'Critique of the Gotha programme', reprinted in Bottomore, T.B. and Rubel, M. (eds) (1963). *Karl Marx. Selected Writings in Sociology and Social Philosophy*. Harmondsworth, Penguin.

Marx, K. (1887). *Capital Vol. 1* (1961 edn). Moscow, Foreign Languages Publishing House.

Marx, K. (1977a). 'Thesis on Feuerbach', in McLellan, D. (ed.). *Karl Marx: Selected Writings*. Oxford, Oxford University Press.

Marx, K. (1977b). 'The Eighteenth Brumaire of Louis Bonaparte', in McLellan, D. (ed.). *Karl Marx: Selected Writings*. Oxford, Oxford University Press.

Marx, K. and Engels, F. (1888). *Manifesto of the Communist Party (1952 edn)*. Moscow, Progress Publishers.

Masterson, A. (1982). *A Place of My Own*. Leicester, National Association of Youth Clubs.

Matthews, J.E. (1966). *Working with Youth Groups*. London, University of London Press.

McBeath, J. (1986). 'The organization of social education', in Brown, C.

et al. (eds). *Social Education: Principles and Practice*. Lewes, Falmer Press.

McLeod, H. (1984). *Religion and the Working Class in Nineteenth Century Britain*. London, Macmillan.

Mill, J.S. (1867). *Inaugural Address as Rector of St Andrews University*. St Andrews, University of St Andrews.

Mills, C.W. (1970). *The Sociological Imagination*. Harmondsworth, Penguin.

Milson, F. (1970). *Youth Work in the 1970's*. London, Routledge and Kegan Paul.

Ministry of Education (1945). *The Purpose and Content of the Youth Service. A Report of the Youth Advisory Council appointed by the Minister of Education in 1943*. London, HMSO.

Ministry of Education (1949). *Report of the Committee on the Recruitment, Training and Conditions of Service of Youth Leaders and Community Centre Wardens (The Jackson Report)*. London, HMSO.

Mishra, R. (1984). *The Welfare State in Crisis. Social Thought and Social Change*. Brighton, Wheatsheaf Books.

Montagu, L. (1904). 'The girl in the background', in Urwick, E.J. (ed.). *Studies in Boy Life in our Cities*. London, Dent.

Moore, M. (1983). 'The Individual Adult Learner', in Tight, M. (ed.) *Education for Adults Vol. 1: Adult Learning and Education*. London, Croom Helm.

Morgan, A.E. (1939). *The Needs of Youth. A Report made to the King George's Jubilee Trust Fund*. Oxford, Oxford University Press.

Morris, R.J. (1979). *Class and Class Consciousness in the Industrial Revolution 1780–1850*. London, Macmillan.

Morrissett, I. and Williams, A.M. (eds) (1981). *Social/Political Education in Three Countries*. Boulder, Colorado, Social Science Education Consortium/ERIC.

Muncie, J. (1984). *'The Trouble with Kids Today'. Youth and Crime in Postwar Britain*. London, Hutchinson.

Musgrove, F. (1964). *Youth and the Social Order*. London, Routledge and Kegan Paul.

NISW (1982). *Social Workers, Their Role and Tasks (The Barclay Report)*. London, Bedford Square Press.

NIYWA (1987). *Social Education in Practice*. Belfast, Standing Conference of Youth Organizations.

National Association of Girls' Clubs (1943). *Annual Report 1943*. London, National Association of Girls' Clubs.

National Association of Youth Clubs (1981). *Submission to the Youth Service Review*. Leicester, National Association of Youth Clubs.

National Youth Bureau (1975, 1983). *Curriculum Development in the Youth Club*. Leicester, National Youth Bureau.

Nava, M. (1984). 'Youth Service provision, social order and question of girls', in McRobbie, A. and Nava, M. (eds). *Gender and Generation*. London, Macmillan.

Newnham, A. (1986). *Employment, Unemployment and Black People*. London, Runnymede Trust.

O'Connor, J. (1973). *The Fiscal Crisis of the State*. London, Macmillan.

O'Higgins, M. (1985). 'Welfare, redistribution, and inequality', in Bean, P. et al. (eds). *In Defence of Welfare*. London, Tavistock.

Opie, I. and Opie, P. (1969). *Children's Games in Street and Playground*. Oxford, Oxford University Press.

Paneth, M. (1944). *Branch Street*. London, George Allen and Unwin.

Pearson, G. (1975). *The Deviant Imagination: Psychiatry, Social Work and Social Change*. London, Macmillan.

Pearson, G. (1983). *Hooligan. A History of Respectable Fears*. London, Macmillan.

Pelham, T.W.H. (1889). *Handbook to Youths' Institutes and Working Boys Clubs*. London, James Nisbet.

Percival, A.C. (1951). *Youth Will Be Led. The Story of the Voluntary Youth Organizations*. London, Collins.

Pethick, E. (1898). 'Working Girls Clubs', in Reason, W. (ed.). *University and Social Settlements*. London, Methuen.

Pfeiffer J.W. and Jones J.E. (1969). *A Handbook of Structured Experiences for Human Relations Training*. San Jose, University Associates.

Piaget, J. (1932). *The Moral Judgement of the Child*. New York, Harper and Row.

Pollock, L.A. (1983). *Forgotten Children: Parent Child Relations from 1500-1900*. Cambridge, Cambridge University Press.

Popple, K. (1988). 'Youth work and race', in Jeffs, T. and Smith, M. (eds). *Young People, Inequality and Youth Work*. London, Macmillan (in press).

Pring, R. (1984). *Personal and Social Education in the Curriculum*. London, Hodder and Stoughton.

Ramdin, R. (1987). *The Making of the Black Working Class in Britain*. Aldershot, Wildwood House.

Rawls, J. (1972). *A Theory of Justice*. Oxford, Clarendon Press.

Reeves, F. and Chevannes, M. (1984). 'The political education of young blacks in Britain'. *Educational Review*, **38** (2).

Rennie, J., Lunzer, E.A. and Williams, W.T. (1974). *Social Education: An Experiment in Four Secondary Schools*. London, Evans.

Rentoul, J. (1987). *The Rich Get Richer. The Growth of Inequality in Britain in the 1980s*. London, Unwin.

Ritchie, N. (1986). *An Inspector Calls. A Critical Review of Her Majesty's Inspectorate Reports on Youth Provision*. Leicester, National Youth Bureau.

Roberts, K. (1983). *Youth and Leisure*. London, George Allen and Unwin.

Roberts, K., White, G.E. and Parker, H.J. (1974). *The Character-training Industry. Adventure Training Schemes in Britain*. Newton Abbot, David and Charles.

Roberts, R. (1973). *The Classic Slum. Salford Life in the First Quarter of the Century*. Harmondsworth, Penguin.

Robins, D. and Cohen, P. (1978). *Knuckle Sandwich. Growing up in the Working Class City*. Harmondsworth, Penguin.

Rogers, A. (1982). *Recording and Reporting*. Leicester, National Association of Youth Clubs.

Rogers, C. (1967). *On Becoming a Person. A Therapist's View of Psychotherapy*. London, Constable.

Rogers, C. (1969). *Freedom to Learn*. Westerville, Ohio, Merrill.

Rogers, C. (1973). *Client Centred Therapy*. London, Constable.

Rogers, J. and Groombridge, B. (1976). *Right to Learn. The Case for Adult Equality*. London, Arrow Books.

Rojek, C. (1985). *Capitalism and Leisure Theory*. London, Tavistock.

Rooff, M. (1935). *Youth and Leisure. A Survey of Girls Organizations in England and Wales*. Edinburgh, Carnegie United Kingdom Trust.

Rosenthal, M. (1986). *The Character Factory. Baden Powell and the Origins of the Boy Scout Movement*. London, Collins.

Rousseau, J.-J. (1911). *Emile*. London, Dent.

Rowntree, B.S. (1941). *Poverty and Progress*. London. Longman.

Russell, C.E.B. (1905). *Manchester Boys, Sketches of Manchester Lads at Work and Play*. Manchester, Neil Richardson (reprint 1984).

Russell, C.E.B. and Rigby, L.M. (1908). *Working Lads' Clubs*. London, Macmillan.

Rutherford, A. (1986). *Growing Out of Crime. Society and Young People in Trouble*. Harmondsworth, Penguin.

Rutter, M. (1979). *Changing Youth in a Changing Society. Patterns of Adolescent Development and Disorder*. Nuffield, Nuffield Provincial Hospital Trust.

Salter, B. and Tapper, T. (1981). *Education, Politics and the State. The Theory and Practice of Educational Change*. London, Grant McIntyre.

Sarup, M. (1986). *The Politics of Multiracial Education*. London, Routledge and Kegan Paul.

Scene (1987). 'Youth Service to get higher profile'. *Scene*, 135.

Scott, C. (1908). *Social Education*. Boston, Ginn and Co.

Scottish Community Education Centre (1982). *Social Education: Methods and Resources*. Edinburgh, Scottish Community Education Centre.

Shaw, K. *et al.* (1988). 'Local Government and youth work. The consequences of declining local autonomy', in Jeffs, T. and Smith, M. (eds) *Welfare and Youth Work Practice*. London, Macmillan (in press).

Simon, B. (1965). *Education and the Labour Movement 1870–1920*. London, Lawrence and Wishart.

Slaughter, J.W. (1911). *The Adolescent*. London, G. Allen.

Smith, D. (1965). 'Front-line organization of the State mental hospital'. *Administrative Science Quarterly*, 10, 381–99.

Smith, D.I. (1979). *Local Authority Expenditure on the Youth Service, 1975–80*. Leicester, National Youth Bureau.

Smith, D.I. (1980). *Local Authority Expenditure on the Youth Service, 1979/80 to 1980/81*. Leicester, National Youth Bureau.

Smith, D.I. (1985). *Expenditure on the Youth Service 1978 to 1983. A Con-*

sultative Document. Leicester, National Youth Bureau.

Smith, D.I. (1987). *Reshaping the Youth Service. Policy Developments Following the Thompson Report*. Leicester, National Youth Bureau.

Smith, M. (1980, 1982). *Creators not Consumers. Rediscovering Social Education*. Leicester, National Association of Youth Clubs.

Smith, M. (1984). *Questions for Survival. Some Problems of Political Education and How to Combat Them*. Leicester, National Association of Youth Clubs.

Smith, M. (1987). *Political Education. Approaches in the Community. Occasional Paper No. 4*. Newcastle, Youth and Policy.

Smith, M.B. (1985). 'The metaphorical basis of selfhood', in Marsella, A.J. et al. (eds). *Culture and Self. Asian and Western Perspectives*. London, Tavistock.

Smith, N. (1984). *Youth Service Provision for Girls and Young Women*. Leicester, National Association of Youth Clubs.

Spence, J. (1988). 'Youth work and gender', in Jeffs, T. and Smith, M. (eds). *Young People, Inequality and Youth Work*. London, Macmillan (in press).

Spradley, J.P. (1980). *The Ethnographic Interview*. New York, Holt Rinehart and Winston.

Spradley, J.P. (1980). *Participant Observation*. New York, Rinehart and Winston.

Springhall, J. (1977). *Youth, Empire and Society. British Youth Movements 1883-1940*. London, Croom Helm.

Springhall, J. (1986). *Coming of Age. Adolescence in Britain 1860-1960*. Dublin, Gill and Macmillan.

Springhall, J., Fraser, B. and Hoare, M. (1983). *Sure and Stedfast. A History of the Boys Brigade 1883-1983*. London, Collins.

Stanley, M. (1878). *Work About the Five Dials*. London, Macmillan.

Stanley, M. (1890). *Clubs for Working Girls*. London, Macmillan.

Stedman Jones, G. (1983). *Languages of Class. Studies in English Working Class History 1832-1982*. Cambridge, Cambridge University Press.

Stedman Jones, G. (1984). *Outcast London. A Study in Relationships Between Classes in Victorian Society* (2nd edn). Harmondsworth, Penguin.

Stenhouse, L. (1975). *An Introduction to Curriculum Research and Development*. London, Heinemann.

Stone, C. (1987). 'Youth workers as caretakers', in Jeffs, T. and Smith, M. (eds). *Youth Work*. London, Macmillan.

Stone, M. (1981). *The Education of the Black Child. The Myth of Multicultural Education*. London, Fontana.

Sweatman, A. (1863). 'Youth Clubs and Institutes', reproduced in Booton, F. (ed.) (1985). *Studies in Social Education, Vol. 1 1860-1890*. Hove, Benfield Press.

Taylor, J. (1972). *From Self Help to Glamour. Working Men's Clubs 1860-1972*. Oxford, History Workshop.

Taylor, T. (1987). 'Youth workers as character builders. Constructing a socialist alternative', in Jeffs, T. and Smith, M. (eds). *Youth Work*. London, Macmillan.

Taylor-Gooby, P. (1985). *Public Opinion, Ideology and State Welfare*. London, Routledge and Kegan Paul.

Thane, P. (1981). 'Childhood in history', in King, M. (ed.). *Childhood Welfare and Justice*. London, Batsford.

Thane, P. (1982). *The Foundations of the Welfare State*. Harlow, Longman.

Thomas, D.N. (1983). *The Making of Community Work*. London, George Allen and Unwin.

Thomas, D.N. (1986). *White Bolts Black Locks. Participation in the Inner City*. London, George Allen and Unwin.

Thomas, M. and Perry, J. (1975). *National Voluntary Youth Organisations*. London, Political and Economic Planning.

Thompson, E.P. (1968). *The Making of the English Working Class*. Harmondsworth, Penguin.

Thompson, K. (1986). *Beliefs & Ideology*. London, Tavistock.

Thompson, P. (1975). *The Edwardians. The Remaking of British Society*. London, Weidenfeld and Nicolson.

Times Educational Supplement (1940). Editorial, 29 June.

Tinker, A. (1981). *The Elderly in Modern Society*. Harlow, Longman.

Townsend, P. and Davidson, N. (1982). *Inequalities in Health*. Harmondsworth, Penguin.

Trenchard, L. and Warren, H. (1985). *Talking about Youth Work*. London, London Gay Teenage Group.

Urwick, E.J. (ed.) (1904). *Studies of Boy Life in our Cities*. London, Dent.

Vicinus, M. (1985). *Independent Women. Work and Community for Single Women*. London, Virago.

Walker, S. and Meighan, R. (1981). 'The hidden curriculum of language', in Meighan, R. (ed.). *A Sociology of Educating*. Eastbourne, Holt, Rinehart and Winston.

Wallman, S. (1984). *Eight London Households*. London, Tavistock.

Walsh, M. (1982). *The Chief Scout's Closing Address to the National Commissioners Conference 1982*. London, The Scout Association.

Walvin, J. (1982). *A Child's World. A Social History of Childhood 1800-1914*. Harmondsworth, Penguin.

Ward, J. (1948). *Children out of School*. London, Central Advisory Council for Education.

Watkins, O. (1972). *Professional Training for Youth Work. The Development of Methods used at the National College for the Training of Youth Leaders 1960-70*. Leicester, Youth Service Information Centre.

Weale, A. (1983). *Political Theory and Social Policy*. London, Macmillan.

Welsh Office (1986). *Report by H.M. Inspectors on Youth Wings in West Glamorgan*. Cardiff, Welsh Office.

White, J. (1980). *Rothschild Buildings. Life in an East End Tenement Block 1887-1920*. London, Routledge and Kegan Paul.

White, J. (1982). *The Aims of Education Restated*. London, Routledge and Kegan Paul.

Whyte, W.F. (1955). *Street Corner Society* (2nd edn). Chicago, University of Chicago Press.

Widdowson, J. (1986). 'Immigration', in Newham History Workshop. *A Marsh and a Gasworks: One Hundred Years of Life in West Ham*. Newham, Newham Parents' Centre.

Wild, P. (1979). 'Recreation in Rochdale, 1900–40'. in Clarke, J. *et al.* (eds). *Working Class Culture*. London, Hutchinson.

Wilding, P. (1982). *Professional Power and Social Welfare*. London, Routledge and Kegan Paul.

Williams, L. (1988). *Partial Surrender. Black Youth and the Youth Service*. Brighton, Falmer Press.

Williams, R. (1976). *Keywords. A Vocabulary of Culture and Society*. London, Fontana.

Willis, P. (1977). *Learning to Labour*. Farnborough, Saxon House.

Willis, P. *et al.* (1985). *The Social Condition of Young People in Wolverhampton in 1984*. Wolverhampton, Wolverhampton Borough Council.

Wilson, E. (1983). 'Feminism and social policy', in Loney, M., Boswell, D. and Clarke, J. (eds). *Social Policy and Social Welfare*. Milton Keynes, Open University Press.

Wilson, P. (1985). *Gutter Feelings. Youth Work in the Inner-city*. Basingstoke, Marshalls.

Woods, P. (1979). *The Divided School*. London, Routledge and Kegan Paul.

Wright, P. (1985). *On Living in an Old Country. The National Past in Contemporary Britain*. London, Verso.

Wringe, C. (1984). *Democracy, Schooling and Political Education*. London, George Allen and Unwin.

YMCA National College (1986). 'Adulthood', in Certificate in Youth & Community Work, *Individuals* SP6. London, YMCA National College.

Yarnitt, M. (1980). 'Second chance to learn, Liverpool; class and adult education', in Thompson, J.L. (ed.). *Adult Education for a Change*. London, Hutchinson.

Index